G000245608

THE
FLEETING
YEARS

ODES OF HORACE

from the Augustan Age of Rome

A new verse translation
with introduction and notes

by
STUART LYONS

Staffordshire University Press

College Road

Stoke-on-Trent

ST4 2DE

First published 1996 by Staffordshire University Press

© Stuart Lyons 1996

ISBN 1-897898-25-8

This book is sold subject to the condition that
it shall not, by way of trade or otherwise, be lent,
re-sold, hired out or otherwise circulated without
the publisher's prior consent in any form of
binding other than that in which it is published
and without a similar condition including this
condition being imposed on the subsequent
purchaser.

Typeset by Staffordshire University Press

Telephone 01782 294000

Fax 01782 744035

To Ellen

*"Dulce ridentem Lalagen amabo,
dulce loquentem."*

"Alas, the fleeting years slip by,
And wrinkles and insistent age
Won't be delayed by piety."

HORACE: Ode II.14

To Charles:

"nunc pede libero
pulsanda tellus"   (I.37)

with my thanks.

Stuart James

4th February 1997.

Foreword by Sir Jeremy Morse KCMG

Horace is one of the great poets of the world. He is in many ways an unusual poet, especially in his four books of Odes.

Consider first what makes their music, for he called them "songs". The Romans of the Augustan age, powerful as they were, were nonetheless dazzled by Greek culture. Their poets sought to fit the Latin language, with its strong word-stress, not to its natural rhythms, which are similar to those of English, but to alien Greek verse-patterns of long and short syllables. We can see how Virgil achieved this with the epic hexameter, and Ovid with the elegiac couplet; but Horace took on a far more formidable task in trying to do the same with the lyric metres of Alcaeus and Sappho. It is impossible now to be certain how the Odes would have sounded when recited, to recreate the counterpoint of verse-stress and word-stress. That he was successful is clear from his fame; at the same time we can note that no later poet developed his metres, or even followed them except in conscious imitation. For us Horace's music may lie in his fine choice of words and – something in which Latin allows much more choice than most modern languages – of word-order.

There are other features which add to the fascination of his poetry. The world of the Odes is peopled with a mixture of mythical, historic, obscure and fictitious characters, not always easily distinguished. The style is pithy, and the train of thought demands attention, as he moves rapidly among his favourite topics of morality and love, drinking and death. The antitheses and oxymorons that ornament his style are mirrored in his own complex poetic character – the moralist who on occasion likes to play the fool, the freedman's son who can sound the imperial trumpet.

All this might make the newcomer think that Horace was a poet for school teachers and scholars – and that would be partly right. As Stuart Lyons says in his Introduction, "Within a hundred years of his death, his odes had become a standard text for study throughout the Roman Empire." They have remained so to this day, and many pupils who have managed to navigate their way through Caesar's "Gallic War" have foundered on the rocks of Horace's Odes.

And yet... despite these rocks, and beyond the barrier of a dead language, Horace is the most companionable of great poets, revealing much of himself, and winning not only the admiration but also the affection of most who have known him over the past 2000 years. In our day we commemorate Virgil, his friend and equal in poetry, with lectures and exhibitions. In contrast, the Horatian Society dines each year in London, and hears two speeches, one by an academic and one by a layman, in a feast of wit and wine.

How quotable he is on these occasions. But like all great poets he has also left his mark on our everyday language – with Latin tags, like *sub judice*, *in medias res* and *nil desperandum*; with inventions that have become English tags, like "purple patch" and "when Homer nods"; with sharp observations like *Naturam expellas furca tamen usque recurret* ("drive Nature out with a pitchfork, and she will run right back"), and *parturiunt montes, nascetur ridiculus mus* ("mountains are in labour: born will be a laughable little mouse"); and, from the Odes themselves, with mighty lines like *dulce et decorum est pro patria mori* ("sweet and glorious it is to die for one's country") and the source of this book's title, *eheu fugaces, Postume, Postume, labuntur anni* ("ah Postumus, Postumus, the fleeting years slip by").

So Horace appeals to all sorts of men and women, including academics. His blend of practical wisdom and verbal economy is particularly attractive to men of affairs, like the author of this book. And both sides of his poetry appeal to the translator; his difficulties and his felicities offer a combined challenge which has attracted hundreds of them over the centuries. The first into English was Lewis Evans, who translated his Satires in 1565; and by 1621 John Ashmore was able to publish a collection entitled "Certain Selected Odes of Horace Englisht". Since then Ben Jonson, Milton, Cowley and Housman are a few of those who have tried their hands on individual Odes, I.5 and IV.7 being among the most popular.

Not so many have translated all 103 Odes. This is a big task; and Stuart Lyons' version, with its accompanying introduction and notes, brings it off in fine style. It will enable poetry lovers without the language to drink from the Horatian spring, and I hope that it may inspire some to learn or brush up their Latin. It is at once magisterial and enlightening, and as Horace himself said:

> *omne tulit punctum qui miscuit utile dulci,*
> *lectorem delectando pariterque monendo*

> " He has gained every point who has mingled profit with pleasure,
>   By delighting and instructing the reader in equal measure."

Jeremy Morse

Note by Christine E King, Professor of History and Vice-Chancellor of Staffordshire University

It is so appropriate that this book is the first to be published under the imprint of Staffordshire University Press. It is the result of the scholarship of a valued member of our Board of Governors, and it embodies everything that this university stands for. The beauty and quality of the works of Horace have been enhanced by the sensitive and creative translation, which has resulted in a collection that is as readable and thought provoking today as it was when it was written two thousand years ago. Academic endeavour of whatever kind is the lifeblood of Staffordshire University, and we too seek to be excellent in everything we do. Education opens minds and the continuous extension of knowledge through academic research is central to the existence of human kind. That we have the opportunity to learn from our predecessors is thanks to scholars such as Stuart Lyons, and we applaud his commitment and ability.

Acknowledgments

Professor David Skilton of the University of Wales Institute of Science and Technology unwittingly caused me to embark on this project. Professor Max Byrd of the University of California gave me the consistent encouragement to see it through. I received much encouragement and valuable advice from Ann Linscott of Royal Doulton and her husband Professor Brian Fender, former Vice-Chancellor of Keele University. Above all, I am indebted to Professor Christine King, the Vice-Chancellor of Staffordshire University, for her support, enthusiasm and commitment to the project and for her suggestion that the Staffordshire University Press should publish it.

Colin Sydenham, Secretary of the Horatian Society, made some sensitive suggestions about the Pyrrha ode and generously sent a copy of an early draft of it to Professor David West of Newcastle University, whose warm and constructive comments and advice were helpful not only for that ode, but for several others. Dr Peter Jones of Newcastle University, who helps to run *Friends of Classics* and is editor of the association's journal **ad familiares**, played a generous role. Dr Stephen Heyworth of Wadham College, Oxford, made helpful observations on the Soracte ode and *Vixi puellis*. Edward Stern, a recent graduate in English of Trinity College, Cambridge, made useful comments on rhythm and metre. Odes I.14, I.25, I.29 and II.10, were submitted to the *The Classical Outlook,* the journal of the American Classical League, before the Staffordshire University Press offered to publish my work in full. I am grateful to *The Classical Outlook* and its editor Richard LaFleur for their support and for bringing forward their publication of the four odes to coincide with the launch of this book.

Many friends and members of my family helped by reading or listening to early drafts of individual odes, and commenting or asking questions about the meaning or context. These included my parents, Bernard and Lucy Lyons, my children, Adam, Joshua and Sarah Lyons, Kate Wootliff and her husband Stanley, Jean Stern, James Farrant, Nicola Beauman and Hugh Gibson. But it was Ellen, my wife who lived with me through the struggle of translation, patiently advising on every word and nuance, which I brought to her for adjudication, and giving me invaluable guidance on shaping the Introduction. To her this book is dedicated with the last words of the Lalage ode.

Lesley Fox, my personal assistant, dealt valiantly with the tasks of photocopying, binding and distributing drafts, organising production meetings and final proofing, while maintaining the efficiency and morale of my office. Geoff Bridgwood of Staffordshire University Press and his colleagues Jean Abbott and Tim Deville were a creative and talented design team, ably assisted by Thelma Bayles, Una Crumpton and other members of the Design and Print Unit. Kevin Ellard, the University Librarian, brought the project through to publication with imagination and efficiency. Finally, I am most grateful to Sir Jeremy Morse for having written the foreword.

To everyone mentioned, and others, I owe my thanks. The omissions and errors are all mine.

Introduction

When Horace died just over two thousand years ago, he was confident
that he had built a lasting achievement. Some years earlier he had
written:

> "I've made a monument to outlast bronze,
> Rise higher than the pyramid of a king;
> No gnawing rain, no north wind's violence,
> Or countless ranks of years and the fleeing
> Of time could e'er this monument erase.
> I shall not all die: some great part of me
> Will escape Death's goddess. With posthumous praise
> I'll freshly grow, be renewed constantly,
> So long as priest with silent priestess shall
> Climb upwards to the Roman Capitol."
>
> (III.30)

His prophecy was correct. Within a hundred years of his death, his odes
had become a standard text for study throughout the Roman Empire.
Throughout Europe, until the end of the nineteenth century, there was
barely a person of culture who could not quote passages from this master
of the epigram and the polished phrase. Today, when Latin is no longer a
compulsory subject for matriculation, his brilliance is in danger of being
lost to future generations. However, the obvious need for an English
verse translation is not without risk. Only verse can convey the rhythm,
thrust, bite and musicality of the original, but no English translation can
replicate the polish and compactness of Horace's Latin.

As a young man Horace was short, dark-haired, impetuous and a
passionate lover. In middle age, he was referred to by the Roman head of
state Augustus as "a most charming little fellow." In later life, his hair
turned white and he developed a voluminous girth. He was no aristocrat,
but the son of a debt-collector from a modest background who had risen
to become a local banker. Through his wit, humanity and perception, and
his prowess and artistry as a poet, he attracted a devoted group of friends
and admirers, and was made welcome in the highest circles of Augustan
Rome.

His achievement was more than simply poetic, but one of extraordinary
technical and cultural innovation:

> "Humble, I rose to power
> And I became the first of men to sing
> Aeolian odes transposed to Italian verse."
>
> (III.30 cont.)

For Horace succeeded in translating Greek poetic form and metre, which benefitted from all the flexibilities of the classical Greek language, into the more formal structures of Latin, creating a new strength and musicality of diction. He became a model so fine, that later generations of Latin writers were unable to take his achievement forward.

* * *

He was born in 65 BC, the year when Pompey the Great, Julius Caesar and Crassus formed a political alliance in Rome, which became known as the First Triumvirate. The alliance was designed to provide stability in a republic torn by faction, through establishing agreed geographical spheres of influence for the three protagonists. The problem proved insurmountable. Stability in Italy depended on the consent of Rome's military leaders to use the legions externally to protect Rome, and not internally to threaten Italy. When Julius Caesar crossed the Rubicon with his legions in 49 BC, he flouted constitutional convention and forced a declaration of war from the Senate. Although Caesar was victorious, the renewal of civil strife, which he precipitated, did not end until Caesar's adopted son Octavian, having defeated Mark Antony in 31 BC at the Battle of Actium, agreed a constitutional settlement with the Senate three and a half years later, by which time Horace was well into middle age.

Horace's full name was Quintus Horatius Flaccus. He was born in Venusia, a town near the river Aufidus in the Italian province of Apulia, east of Rome. His father was not from a family of long-standing, but, in days when slavery was still prevalent, was a freedman by rank, who became a debt collector, before rising to his position as a local banker. Nothing is known of Horace's mother, and he refers in Ode III.4 to his babyhood in the countryside in the charge of an Apulian nurse.

When Horace reached his teens, his father took him to Rome, where he studied humanities under a teacher of fine repute called Orbilius. From there he was sent to study in Athens, regarded then as the centre of Mediterranean culture and learning. There, if not in Rome, he absorbed the works of the great lyric poets of Greece's past, Pindar, Alcaeus, Sappho and Anacreon. In Athens, as at Rome, he is likely to have studied grammar, rhetoric and advocacy, the normal disciplines in that period. He became well-versed in Greek and Roman myth and religion. He is likely to have travelled to at least some of the tourist destinations referred to in Ode I.7, Rhodes and Mytilene, Ephesus and Corinth, Argos and Mycenae, Sparta and Larisa.

Meanwhile, these were turbulent times at Rome. In Horace's childhood, the capital had basked in the Gallic conquests of Julius Caesar. Then, the First Triumvirate collapsed. Having crossed the river Rubicon, Caesar was challenged by Pompey, who led troops loyal to the Roman Senate.

Horace was at that time sixteen years old and was probably already studying in Rome. In the civil war that followed, Caesar defeated Pompey in 48 BC and two of Pompey's sons in 45 BC.

By force of arms, Caesar became supreme in Rome, to the dismay of traditionalists within the Senate, who saw their power and Rome's ancient values threatened. Brutus was one such person and led the assassination of Julius Caesar in the capital on the Ides of March, or 15 March, 44 BC. Romans were soon bitterly divided into those who supported the act and those who did not. By now, Horace was a young student in Athens. Among the Roman students there, many sided with Brutus, who is likely to have appeared as a champion of the old republic and the integrity of the Senate.

In the jockeying for power which followed the assassination, Brutus, Mark Antony, and Octavius, Caesar's adopted son and great-nephew, all played significant roles. Octavius, learning at the age of eighteen that he was Julius Caesar's principal heir, assumed the name Julius Caesar Octavianus. Nearly sixteen years later, after the constitutional settlement of 27 BC, Octavian, as he is referred to in English writings, was awarded the title of Augustus by the Senate at the prompting of Munatius Plancus, the addressee of Ode I.7. Octavius, Octavian, Caesar Augustus, and Augustus are all the same person.

After Julius Caesar's assassination on the Ides of March 44 BC, the Caesarian party, led by Mark Antony and Octavian, took control in Rome. Brutus and his fellow-conspirator Cassius left Italy. Cassius gathered an army in Syria. Brutus went to Athens, where he formed a cadre of young officers. Horace was one of his recruits and was given the rank of military tribune, a sort of subaltern on the general stafff.

Brutus gathered further recruits in Macedonia and Illyria to meet the expected threat from the Caesarians. This may have provided Horace's first opportunity to experience in northern Greece the winds of Thrace and landscapes of Thessaly, which give rise to some powerful images in his odes. Meanwhile, Mark Antony, Octavian and the forces of the Caesarian alliance avoided a naval blockade in the Adriatic and crossed to Macedonia. There, two years after the assassination, they met Brutus's army at Philippi. Two engagements took place, the second three weeks after the first. These resulted in Brutus's defeat and suicide. In an ode composed many years later, Horace describes to a former comrade-in-arms the ignominy and trauma of the defeat:

> "With you I felt Philippi and swift flight,
>   Ingloriously leaving my small shield,
> When manliness was shattered, and the might
>   Of youth fell chin-first on the shameful field."
>
>   (II.7)

Politics in Rome remained unsettled. Real power lay not in the hands of the Senate and the aristocrats who sat there, but with those who could raise an army. This was not a difficult matter for men of wealth and position, since high political office, in the form of the consulate, usually led to the proconsular governorship of one of Rome's overseas provinces and to the control of the Roman legions posted there. After the Caesarian victory at Philippi, the rivalry between Mark Antony and Octavian surfaced. In 40 BC troops loyal to each had a stand-off outside Brindisi, or Brundisium as it was then known, in south-east Italy. Octavian was saved from possible disaster by two factors. A young Roman commander named Asinius Pollio refused to accept instructions to attack Octavian's troops, insisting on awaiting Mark Antony's arrival; to Pollio, Horace subsequently addressed the first ode of his second book. Second, there was Maecenas. Maecenas, who two years later was to become Horace's patron, was Augustus' friend and adviser, an Etruscan of subtle mind and formidable powers of diplomacy, who seems to have claimed royal ancestry. Maecenas was the architect of the so-called peace of Brundisium, under which it was agreed that Mark Antony should remain in the east, Octavian stay in the west, and a third Caesarian, Lepidus, be given North Africa. So, the Second Triumvirate was established. To Maecenas, Horace was to address the first ode of his first book of odes, when it was published years later in 23 BC:

> "Maecenas, born of ancient royal line,
> Guardian, protector and sweet pride of mine."
>
> (I.1)

The Second Triumvirate was no more successful than the First in securing a lasting peace. Octavian, together with his brilliant general Agrippa, asserted his authority over the western Mediterranean and in 36 BC defeated the dissident son of Pompey the Great, Sextus Pompeius, in a sea battle off Sicily, so regaining control of the island for Rome. But already, Lepidus was embarking on an attempt against Octavian from North Africa. He was soon stripped of power. However, the bounds of the Roman republic were not wide enough to contain the rivalry of Antony and Octavian. Antony, who had been given Octavian's sister Octavia in marriage before departing for the East, became passionately involved with Cleopatra, the queen of Egypt. Rashly, he proposed to give to Cleopatra's sons territories over which the Roman republic fancied its rights. There were other political and personal disputes. The final breach came in 32 BC, when Octavian drove Antony's supporters from Rome. Octavian declared war, not on his fellow-Roman, but on Cleopatra. A sea battle was fought at Actium on 2 September 31 BC. Antony and Cleopatra were defeated and fled to Alexandria. First Antony, then Cleopatra committed suicide. In a dramatic and celebratory poem, Horace describes the end of Cleopatra, "Fate's monster", as the citizens of Rome regarded her, but a monster who faced death with admirable courage:

> "She dared with face serene to see
> Her fallen palace; then bravely
>> Handled her deadly snakes, until
>> Her body drank the poison vile.

> "More fierce when she resolved to die,
> Scorning a jailer's cruel galley,
>> No humble woman, she never sank
>> To grace a proud triumph, stripped of rank."
>>>>> (I.37)

Meanwhile, what of Horace himself? He had returned home under an amnesty after Brutus' defeat at Philippi in 42 BC. He was only 23 years old and was forgiven his impetuosity. He took a position as a junior treasury official, for which his father's banking background suited him. He began to move in a circle of poets, and two of them, Virgil and Varius, introduced him to Maecenas in Rome in 38 BC. Maecenas was an extraordinary individual. He and Marcus Agrippa had remained Octavian's closest associates: Agrippa, disciplined, effective, the apparent quintessence of Roman morality; Maecenas, a brilliant and creative negotiator and, subsequently, civil administrator, a non-Roman of extravagant lifestyle and broad cultural interests. Within two years Maecenas had given Horace a small country estate in the Sabine hills, where Horace spent much of his life until Maecenas' and his own death in 8 BC.

Horace was also introduced to Octavian, by now the most powerful man in Rome. Octavian, seriously or otherwise, offered him a position as private secretary. No doubt he recognised Horace's facility with words. Horace declined. Octavian was not offended. Perhaps, instead, Horace would write a poem celebrating the victories of Octavian's great general Agrippa. Horace penned a refusal, addressed to Agrippa:

> "Too slight for such grand things, my sense of shame
> And Muse that governs an unwarlike lyre
> Bar me from spoiling excellent Caesar's name
>> And yours, through praise my talents can't inspire."
>>>> (I.6)

Horace had, after all, been on the wrong side at Philippi. Octavian remained undisturbed by the elegant rebuff.

The odes themselves show how Horace's relationships with Maecenas and Augustus developed. To Maecenas, Horace offered gratitude for a comfortable and often idyllic country life, and the opportunity to pursue his calling as a lyric poet. For Augustus, Horace's earlier refusal to become a court poet was later reversed. The lyricist, noted for the personal statement and the delicate cameo, added a greater legitimacy and prestige to the regime, when he eventually lent it his talents.

* * *

After Horace was introduced to Maecenas in 38 BC, he blossomed not as a lyric poet, but as a young satirist, writing hexameters in a conversational style. Hexameters had been the metre of Homer in the great Greek epics, the Iliad and the Odyssey, composed many centuries earlier. Epic poetry had been brought to Rome in 272 BC by Livius Andronicus, a Greek from Tarentum in southern Italy, who translated the Odyssey into Latin. Later, Ennius became the composer of the first truly Latin epic, the Annals, but after his death Latin hexameter verse failed to capture the Roman imagination, until it was revitalised in the first century BC by Lucretius in his De Rerum Natura, or On the Nature of Things, a fine and imaginative work in six books. Virgil then adopted hexameters for his Eclogues, poems on bucolic themes published in 37 BC, and brought them to their finest expression in his Georgics and in his great epic, the Aeneid.

Hexameter verse was the medium which Horace adopted, with wit, ribaldry and pace, to write a series of discourses and satires, which he called "*sermones*" but are known in English as the "Satires". The first book of Satires was published in 35 BC. It included poems on the subject of wealth, sex and friendship, as well as an account of a journey to Brindisi with Maecenas and Virgil in 37 BC, when they supposedly covered about 230 miles in fifteen days. Five years later, the second book of Satires was published, which includes a touching poem of thanks to Maecenas for the gift of the Sabine farm (Sat.II.6), thanks which were later repeated in the odes.

It appears from the evidence of his writings that, during the thirties, Horace maintained some of his treasury duties and that he had a full social life in Rome. His girl friends were often of Greek or Thracian background and had presumably come to Rome to share in the wealth and excitement of the metropolis. They included musicians and ladies of leisure and pleasure, but not girls from distinguished Roman families, who were well-protected until marriage, and who were married early to men of similar wealth and breeding. Horace, the freedman's son, never married, but his sexuality was not in doubt. "Of girls till now I'd never tire, I fought campaigns not without glory," was his boast in later years (III.26) and his bedroom was said to be covered with mirrors. About one quarter of the odes concern loves and lovers, or touch on them. In perhaps the most beautiful love-duet of Latin literature, a former girl-friend contrasts her present lover with Horace:

> "Though he's more beautiful than a star,
>> And you lighter than cork, and more angry
> Than the rough sea of Hadria,
>> With you I'd love to live and gladly die."

(III.9)

The circle of poets around Maecenas, including Virgil, Varius and Tibullus, was another focus of Horace's social life. Drinking parties with friends were a regular means of entertainment, and a source of fun and gossip. If time permitted, Horace would move around the seamier parts of the city to observe local character and patterns of speech.

As Rome settled into a period of domestic peace, Horace put hexameter verse temporarily aside, and turned to new rhythms based on Greek models. In 29 BC he published the Epodes, almost all of which were written in couplets with iambic or dactylic metres. The word epode refers to a form of lyric metre invented by Archilochus, in which a longer verse is followed by a shorter. There were seventeen epodes in Horace's book, containing humour, satire and invective, together with observations on love and politics. This was Horace's mid-stage between hexameters and the polished lyric poetry of the Odes. The period between 29 BC and 23 BC, when the first three books of Horace's Odes were published, marks the high point of his development, just as it marks the initial consolidation of Augustus' position as head of the Roman state, and the peak of Maecenas' career as Augustus' political adviser and urban administrator in Rome.

It was a happy period for Horace. Increasingly, he spent time on the small estate which Maecenas had given him in the Sabine hills above Tibur, east of Rome. He found the countryside, with its sounding springs, its woodlands and rivers, irresistible. Nothing he had seen in Greece, he declared, had ever struck him

> "so much as the home
> Of resonant Albunea or the foam
> Of hurtling Anio or Tibur's lush wood
> And orchards where the mobile rivulets flood."

(I.7)

And there was the farm itself, perched high in the hills, with a tall pine-tree standing above the farm-house (III.22), valleys and polished rocks below, and goats wandering all around (I.17). Why suppose, he asked,

> "That I would want to build in the latest style
> A hill-top palace with a swanky gate?
> Why would I wish to change my Sabine vale
> For riches that were more elaborate?"

(III.1)

In landscapes like these, one could harvest the day and forget concerns about the future (I.11); one could lie in the long grass under the shade of the poplar and the pine, as a shimmering brook laboured below:

> "Here send for wines and perfumes sweet,
> The flowers of the rose soon dead,
> While age and circumstance permit
> And the three Fates spin out their thread."
>
> (II.3)

* * *

After his victory over Mark Antony at Actium and the subsequent suicides of Antony and Cleopatra in Alexandria, Octavianus Caesar, as the victor was still known, spent the year 30 BC in the east, securing the frontiers of empire and the allegiance of the local populations and their rulers. In the summer of 29 BC he returned to Rome a hero. On three successive days, at the invitation of the Senate, he led triumphal processions through the city, in celebration of his victories over the forces of the East in Illyria, at Actium and in Alexandria. The Temple of Divine Julius was dedicated at about this time in honour of the dead dictator, Julius Caesar, a dedication which had resonances for his godlike heir. The following year the Senate, continuing to break precedent, appointed Octavian consul for the fourth successive year since 31 BC and the sixth time to that date. His prestige was enormous. In the autumn of 28 BC his magnificent new Temple of Apollo was consecrated on the Palatine Hill. One might ask who was the sun-god, Apollo or Octavian, but Horace, in a poem composed for the occasion, confined himself to a more personal style of prayer:

> "Grant, o Latona's son,
> That in good health and, I pray,
> With an unimpaired mind I may
> Enjoy the things I have won,
>
> "And grant that I do not mar
> Old age with dishonour, I pray,
> And let me continue to play
> On the strings of my guitar."
>
> (I.31)

The glorification of the prince, the breaking of constitutional precedent and Octavian's control of Rome's overseas forces, created within the state ambiguities and stresses which had to be resolved. On 13 January 27 BC, the first step towards a constitutional settlement was taken. Octavian restored the Senate and People of Rome to their traditional places at the formal centre of the republic by resigning a number of his powers and the overseas provinces to them. In return, on the proposal of Munatius Plancus, the Senate granted Octavian the title of Augustus.

Now, in the prime of his years, Horace responded to the emergence of the Augustan Age. In his series of Roman Odes, as the first six poems of Book III are called, he spoke out in the Alcaic metre, which he had adapted from Greece, for a return to traditional Roman values and patriotism:

> "Roman, though guiltless, you must now atone
> For your forefathers' crimes, till you remake
> The shrines and temples that are falling down
> And the images polluted with black smoke."
>
> (III.6)

Pointing, in a separate ode, to the horrors of long civil war, he attributed them to declining religious and moral standards:

> "He, who will end this impious age
> Of carnage and of civil rage,
> If he wants statues with the name
> 'Father of Cities', may he tame
> Our unchecked immorality."
>
> (III.24)

* * *

When Octavian received the title Augustus, he was in his mid-thirties. He had not lost his appetite for military glory. He was anxious to preserve peace within the empire by securing its borders. He left Italy within a year of receiving the title and spent three years away, first in Gaul and then in Spain, where he fought a not entirely successful campaign against the Cantabrians in the north. Other expeditions were mounted in the east, by Augustus' legates. Horace, always more human when he exchanged rhetoric for personal statement, maintained, in a touching cameo piece addressed to a young officer, that even victory was not wholly glorious:

> "Which of those foreign girls
> Will serve you when her young love has been slain?
> Which princely boy with oiled and perfumed curls
> Will be assigned to fill your cup again,
> Though he was taught to use his father's bow
> And fire oriental arrows?"
>
> (I.29)

Augustus returned to Italy in the middle of 24 BC. After the euphoria of his return five years earlier, this was a period of political difficulty. There had been many Roman casualties in Spain, Augustus himself was ill and weak, and there appeared to be disquiet among some of the old senatorial families about a perceived loss of position. Not all the facts are known. Contemporary writers may have considered it inadvisable to record them. However, there was a crisis. Marcus Primus, a proconsular governor in Macedonia, was accused of having made war in Thrace without senatorial authority. At his trial he was defended by Varro Murena, the brother of Maecenas' wife Terentia and the half-brother of Proculeius of Ode II.2. Murena, who may have been the augur toasted by Horace in Ode III.19, had recently been appointed consul. He was a man of hot temper and hasty actions, which has persuaded many scholars, in an area where evidence is complex and uncertain, but probably persuasive, that he was the Licinius whom Horace had warned:

"Your life would be in better shape,
   If you stopped pressing out to sea,
   Or clinging too close to the rocky cape
   While eyeing storms so warily."

(II.10)

Murena, if it was he, did not take the poet's advice. He defended his client by accusing Augustus. It was Augustus, he claimed, together with Augustus' young nephew Marcellus, who had given his client the necessary authority to embark on hostilities. Augustus came to court to deny the accusation. Primus was convicted. Murena, angry, allowed himself to become involved in a conspiracy. Maecenas, the patron of Horace and chief adviser of Augustus, could not resist warning his delightful wife Terentia, thought possibly to have been the Licymnia of Horace's Ode II.12, that her brother's life was in danger. One could understand Maecenas' indiscretion, particularly if his wife was the "true heart for love shared so well" of whom Horace had written:

"How neatly she can dance, and play
   Her jokes and games, and throw her arms
   Round girls glowing with youthful charms
   On thronged Diana's holiday."

(II.12)

Augustus was less sympathetic. After he learned of Maecenas' indiscretion, his political confidence in him never recovered, although socially the breach seems eventually to have been repaired. Murena himself was killed, so it was reported, trying to avoid arrest.

Calpurnius Piso was appointed consul to replace Murena and at this point Augustus' health broke down completely. Believing himself to be on the point of death, he handed his state papers to Piso and his signet ring to his closest associate Agrippa, the winner of six military victories and the builder of Augustan Rome.

Augustus recovered, saved apparently by a regime of cold baths, but he resigned his consulate to Lucius Sestius. So, when the first three books of the Odes were published later in 23 BC, Maecenas was honoured with the dedicatory prologue, Augustus with the ode after that, and the great poet Virgil with the third ode, but it was the newly-promoted Sestius who was honoured by Horace as the addressee of the Spring Ode, which, after the recent troubles, began felicitously:

> "Keen winter melts, the pleasant time of spring
>   Has come in its due turn, the west wind blows,
> And from the shipyards engines start to bring
>   The dry hulls down to where the water flows."
>   (I.4)

* * *

Horace's fourth and final book of odes was not published until 13 BC, ten years after the first three volumes. These had been published during a period of tension in Rome, when Augustus' supremacy had to be re-established and Maecenas had lost his pre-eminent position as Augustus' chief adviser. Perhaps these events led to a loss of confidence among Horace and his circle; once Maecenas' power had declined, the flamboyant lifestyle of their patron might have been less acceptable. Perhaps the odes were not so well received as Horace had hoped; intended for the urbane and well-educated, they were, in the main, not the stuff of easy or instant popularity. Perhaps Horace simply felt the need for a change of idiom.

At any rate, during the next three years, from 23 to 20 BC, Horace returned to his cheerful hexameters and wrote the first book of the Epistles, consisting of twenty poems of varying length. In the very first poem, he addressed Maecenas and announced that he was giving up lyric poetry. "Age and mind have changed," he declared. The Epistles reflected an easy philosophy of middle age, the security and comfort of the Sabine farm, but also a concern about declining health and vigour.

From the year 20 BC Horace's poetic output almost ceased. His fellow poets Virgil and Tibullus died. Maecenas' political career was over, though cordiality with Augustus had been restored. Towards Horace, however, the emperor remained an affectionate admirer. In 17 BC, Augustus, by now head of a mainly peaceful and well-ordered empire, launched the Centennial Games, a showpiece event designed to present Rome as the capital of the civilised world. Part of the ceremony was to be the *Carmen Saeculare*, a secular or centennial hymn which Horace was to compose. This public recognition from the head of state and the opportunity to have his work performed in front of a vast audience must have been a high point in Horace's life. He began to write odes again and Book IV, a small final collection of fifteen pieces, was published in 13 BC. In Ode IV.3, he remarks on his recognised status as "minstrel of the Roman lyre"; "Now envy's tooth will gnaw me less," he writes. His Hymn to Apollo, turns into a rehearsal for the *Carmen Saeculare* itself:

> "Observe the Sapphic metre and the beating
> On my guitar of this, your master's thumb."
> (IV.6)

Horace concludes the Hymn to Apollo with a proud reminder to the young girls who sing in the chorus:

> "When you are wed, you'll say, 'For the gods above,
> When the new century brought festive days,
> I once performed a hymn which they did love,
> And I was tutored by the bard Horace.' "

After the games, Augustus pressed Horace to write odes in honour of the imperial family, the Augustan age and Augustus himself. Many years had passed since Horace's refusal to Agrippa in Ode I.6. Now in his fifties, the last decade of his life, the poet revealed that he had become a committed Augustan. In this final book of odes, the freshness of expression had gone, but the craftsmanship remained, accompanied by a profound gratitude for the Augustan peace and a commitment to the regime. Horace celebrated the Alpine victories of Augustus' stepsons Drusus and Tiberius in Ode IV.4; Augustus and the Augustan peace in the following ode; the homage paid to Augustus by the far-flung nations of the world in the penultimate ode; and, in the last ode of all, the Augustan Age itself:

> "With Caesar as our institutions' guard,
> No civil rage or force will drive out peace;
> No, nor the anger which hammers out the sword
> And brings hostilities to sad cities...

> "Surrounded by the bounties Liber gives,
>   We, both on common and on holy day,
> Together with our children and our wives,
>   After we first to heaven with due rites pray,

> "Will sing how, with their fathers' attributes,
>   Our princes have the crown of virtue won,
> And then, accompanied by Lydian flutes,
>   Of Troy, Anchises and kind Venus' son."
>   (IV.15)

This was the last of Horace's odes. A second book of Epistles emerged a short time later, containing just three hexameter poems, including the Epistle to Piso, commonly known as the Art of Poetry.

*   *   *

By now Horace was in his declining years. Maecenas, his friend and patron of thirty years, predeceased him by a few weeks. The poet's prophecy, made years before at the time of one of Maecenas' illnesses, was brought to fruition:

> "We shall go, shall go
> Wherever you shall lead; and we'll follow
> Our supreme journey, comrades well-prepared."
>   (II.17)

Suetonius the historian records that Horace died on 27 November in the year when Marcius Censorinus (the addressee of Ode IV.8) was consul with Asinius Gallus. It was 8 BC and Horace was just approaching his fifty-seventh birthday when a severe illness struck. Too weak to have a will prepared, the poet named Augustus as his heir. Horace was buried at the side of the Esquiline Hill in Rome, close to Maecenas' tomb.

Horace's formal epitaph is the epilogue to Book III with which this introduction begins. His philosophical epitaph is perhaps contained in the Ode to Postumus:

> "Alas, the fleeting years slip by,
>   And wrinkles and insistent age
> Won't be delayed by piety,
>   Nor death that no man can assuage."

He continues three stanzas later:

> "We must leave our house, the land we till,
> Our pleasing wife; of these trees we tend
> None but the hated cypress will
> Follow their brief lord to the end."

Many poets would have ended there, but Horace would not have been Horace without a sting in the tail. Adjusted to reflect twentieth-century drinking preferences, the ode ends:

> "A worthier heir will quaff the wine
> That with a hundred keys you stored,
> And stain the floor with port too fine
> To be served at a pontiff's board."
>
> (II.14)

Stuart Lyons
July 1996

CONTENTS

Book I

29. **To Iccius**
Do you now covet the Arabs' blessed store
Icci, beatis nunc Arabum invides

30. **Prayer to Venus**
Venus, queen of Cnidos, pray
O Venus, regina Cnidi Paphique

31. **Prayer to Apollo**
What is the bard's behest
Quid dedicatum poscit Apollinem

32. **To the lyre**
We're called. If ever, sitting in the shade
Poscimur. si quid vacui sub umbra

33. **To Tibullus**
Don't ache too much in memory
Albi, ne doleas plus nimio memor

34. **On the divine**
I seldom took the gods too seriously
Parcus deorum cultor et infrequens

35. **To the goddess Fortuna**
O divine ruler of fair Antium
O diva, gratum quae regis Antium

36. **To Numida**
With lyre and incense I'll fulfil my vow
Et ture et fidibus iuvat

37. **The death of Cleopatra**
Now is the time to drink and beat
Nunc est bibendum, nunc pede libero

38. **To a slave boy**
I loathe all lavish Persian decoration
Persicos odi, puer, apparatus

Book II

1. **To Asinius Pollio**
   The civil strife which in the bygone days
   Motum ex Metello consule civicum

2. **To Sallustius Crispus**
   Sallustius Crispus, no colour imbues
   Nullus argento color est avaris

3. **To Dellius**
   Keep a cool head when things are hard
   Aequam memento rebus in arduis

4. **To Xanthias of Phocis**
   You love a slavegirl: do not be ashamed
   Ne sit ancillae tibi amor pudori

5. **To Lalage's admirer**
   Too weak to bear the yoke with subdued neck
   Nondum subacta ferre iugum valet

6. **To Septimius**
   You plan to travel with me to Cadiz
   Septimi, Gadis aditure mecum

7. **To Pompeius Varus**
   Into the hour of death you often came
   O saepe mecum tempus in ultimum

8. **To Barine**
   If any punishment for broken faith
   Ulla si iuris tibi peierati

9. **To Valgius Rufus**
   No, not for ever does the piercing rain
   Non semper imbres nubibus hispidos

10. **To Licinius**
    Your life would be in better shape
    Rectius vives, Licini, neque altum

11. **To Quinctius Hirpinus**
    What the warlike Cantabrians may conspire
    Quid bellicosus Cantaber et Scythes

12. **To Maecenas**
    The long and fierce Numantian war
    Nolis longa ferae bella Numantiae

13. **To a tree**
    Whoever planted you there first
    Ille et nefasto te posuit die

14. **To Postumus**
    Alas, the fleeting years slip by
    Eheu fugaces, Postume, Postume

Book III

1. **The unholy throng**
    I loathe the unholy throng, and I have barred
    Odi profanum vulgus et arceo

2. **"Dulce et decorum"**
    Hardship and poverty let him but bear
    Angustam amice pauperiem pati

3. **Juno's declaration**
    The man who is just and clings to his intent
    Iustum et tenacem propositi virum

4. **In praise of the Muse**
    Come down from heaven, Calliope
    Descende caelo et dic age tibia

5. **The example of Regulus**
    When Jupiter is thundering in the sky
    Caelo tonantem credidimus Iovem

6. **Rome's moral decline**
    Roman, though guiltless, you must now atone
    Delicta maiorum immeritus lues

7. **To Asterie**
    Why do you weep? The fair west wind
    Quid fles, Asterie, quem tibi candidi

8. **To Maecenas**
    What am I doing, you ask, a bachelor
    Martiis caelebs quid agam Kalendis

9. **The poet and Lydia**
    As long as I was your delight
    Donec gratus eram tibi

10. **To Lyce**
    If you drank from the distant Tanais
    Extremum Tanain si biberes, Lyce

11. **To Mercury and the lyre**
    Mercury, who once in Amphion found
    Mercuri, nam te docilis magistro

12. **To Neobule**
    It is not done
    Miserarum est neque amori

13. **The Bandusian spring**
    Spring of Bandusia, more bright than glass
    O fons Bandusiae splendidior vitro

14. **To the common people of Rome**
    Like Hercules, Augustus sought the rewards
    Herculis ritu modo dictus, o plebs

15. **To Chloris**
    You are just a poor man's wife
    Uxor pauperis Ibyci

Book IV

1. **To Venus**
   Venus, are you resuming war
   Intermissa, Venus, diu

2. **To Iullus Antonius**
   Whoever, Iullus, strives to emulate
   Pindarum quisquis studet aemulari

3. **To the Muse**
   He, whom at birth with kindly eye
   Quam tu, Melpomene, semel

4. **In praise of Drusus**
   Like the winged servant of the thunderbolt
   Qualem ministrum fulminis alitem

5. **To Augustus Caesar**
   Born of the good gods, guardian excellent
   Divis orte bonis, optime Romulae

6. **Hymn to Apollo**
   O god, your vengeance at their massive boast
   Dive, quem proles Niobea magnae

7. **To Torquatus**
   The snows have scattered. Now upon the leas
   Diffugere nives, redeunt iam gramina campis

8. **To Censorinus**
   I'd willingly give bowls and gifts of bronze
   Donarem pateras grataque commodus

9. **To Lollius**
   Lest you may think that all my words will die
   Ne forte credas interitura, quae

10. **To Ligurinus**
    Still you are cruel, although the gifts of love
    O crudelis adhuc et Veneris muneribus potens

11. **To Phyllis**
    I've a full jar of Alban wine
    Est mihi nonum superantis annum

12. **To Virgil**
    Now, spring's companions who calm the sea
    Iam veris comites, quae mare temperant

13. **To Lyce**
    The gods have heard my prayers
    Audivere, Lyce, di mea vota, di

Book I

I.1

To Maecenas

Maecenas atavis edite regibus

Maecenas born of ancient royal line,
Guardian, protector and sweet pride of mine,
Some men in racing chariots love to pound
The Olympic dust; their red-hot wheels scrape round
The marker-posts; they win the noble palm,
And earthly lords then gods in heaven become.
One, if a mob of fickle burghers vies
To raise with triple honours, wins his prize;
One, if in his own granary is kept
All that from Libyan threshing-floors is swept.
A man who, glad at heart, applies his hoe
To cleave his father's fields, would never go
To be a trembling mariner afloat
The sea of Myrtos in a Cyprian boat.
The merchant, when the wind from Africa raves
Locking in combat with the Icarian waves,
In trepidation lauds the life of leisure
He spends in his home town, and country pleasure;
But soon his battered ship is in repair,
For poverty he's not been taught to bear!
One man loves goblets of old Massic wine
And steals a long siesta, to recline
Stretched out beneath a green arbutus or
By a slow source of sacred water. More
Enjoy a military camp, the sound
Of trumpet mixed with cornet all around,
And warfare which their mother execrates.
The hunter under freezing heavens waits
Until, as he his tender wife forgets,
A Marsian boar breaks through tight-woven nets
Or faithful hounds a fallow-deer espy.
I am uplifted to the gods on high
By ivy garlands, prizes in the school
Of learned poesy. The woodlands cool,
And Nymphs and Satyrs dancing with light grace,
Divide me from the ordinary race
Of men, if Muse Euterpe plays the flute
And Polyhymnia plucks the Lesbian lute;
But if you count me among the lyric bards,
My head will be so high, I'll hit the stars.

I.2
To Augustus Caesar
Iam satis terrae

Our Father has sent down to earth enough snow
And terrible hail. He has hurled his bolts down
At Rome's holy places, his right hand aglow,
     And frightened the town,

Frightened the people, that Pyrrha's grim time
Will return. In years past she bewailed portents strange:
Old Proteus drove herds from deep ocean to climb
     The high mountain range,

And fishes all clung to the tops of elm-trees
Where turtle-doves had their familiar abode,
And petrified deer swam in cascading seas.
     Yellow Tiber flowed

Just now, as we've seen, with its waves twisted back
In violent motion from the Etruscan shore
To throw royal monuments down in its track
     And to turn o'er

The temple of Vesta. Yes, Tiber, who loves
Sad Ilia, his consort, slips leftward and swanks
He'll avenge her by straying (though Jove disapproves)
     Over his banks.

Youth's numbers are few, through the sins of the father;
They'll hear that our citizens sharpened the sword
Which should have brought death to grim Parthians rather
     Than civil discord.

Which god should our people invoke to arrest a
Collapse of the Empire? With what hymn or prayer
Can our holy virgins wear down divine Vesta
     Unwilling to hear?

Which god will Jove order to expiate our crime?
We pray that with bright shoulders cloaked in a cloud
Prophetic Apollo will come in due time,
     Or, laughing loud,

The goddess of Eryx, around whom cavort
Winged Cupid and Mirth, or our ancestor Mars,
To his spurned race come back, fed up with the sport
     Of long-drawn-out wars,

The cry of the battle-field, helmets afire,
The keen-visaged African footsoldier glaring
At a blood-spattered foe; or you, son of dear Maia,
      Mercury, daring

To fly down and change your own form to the frame
Of a young man on earth, and, braving the danger,
To suffer the people to give you the name
      Of Caesar's avenger.

Do not return heavenward too soon! May you long
Be happy among us and, pray, do not seize
Unfairly upon every fault and each wrong!
      Nor may a breeze

Too swift snatch you up! Here, great triumphs be yours,
May you love the names Father and Prince, and may you
Take your revenge on the Medes and their horse,
      Rome's Caesar new!

I.3
For Virgil
Sic te diva potens Cypri

Venus, over Cyprus reigning,
     Castor, Pollux, brightly shining,
Aeolus, father of the winds,
     Who his other children binds,
If he follows my behest,
     Save Iapyx in the west:
Heavenly gods, guide Virgil's ship,
     Charged to bear him on this trip.
Good ship, also, I implore,
     Bring him safe to Athens' shore;
Keep your promised cargo whole,
     And save half of my own soul.
Oaken heart and brazen chest,
     He who first put to the test
Fragile craft on cruel seas.
     He feared not the African breeze
Battling head-on with the blast
     Of northerlies approaching fast,
Hyades which ill presage
     Or southerly with furious rage,
The Adriatic lord who'll tell
     If to raise or calm the swell.
Death's tread was not feared by him,
     Dry-eyed he saw monsters swim,
Turbulent seas he saw and, worse,
     Epirus' rocks, the sailor's curse.
God, pursuing a vain notion,
     Parts lands with estranging ocean,
But heretical craft still please
     To leap across untouchable seas.
Boldly exploring, mankind's throng
     Dives into forbidden wrong.
Bold Prometheus, by a fraud,
     Brought men fire, an ill reward:
Filched from its etherial home,
     Fire mad cruel consumption come;
A new host of fevers then
     Settled on the lands of men;
The necessity, once late,
     Of distant death, picked up its gait.
Daedalus tried the empty air
     On wings not given man to share;

Hercules broke through Acheron.
           Naught by mortals can't be done:
We in our stupidity
           Try to reach the very sky,
Not allowing, through our faults,
           Jove to still his thunderbolts.

I.4
To Sestius
Solvitur acris hiems

Keen winter melts, the pleasant time of spring
           Has come in its due turn, the west wind blows,
And from the shipyards engines start to bring
           The dry hulls down to where the water flows.

The herd no longer joys in stables warm,
           Nor ploughman in the hot fire's glowing light;
The hoar-frost settles not upon the farm,
           And pastures green no longer turn to white.

Now Cytherean Venus leads the dance,
           The ascending moon illuminates the sky,
And comely Graces with the Nymphs advance,
           Joined hand in hand in perfect modesty.

With left foot, then with right, alternately,
           They shake the earth in rhythm to their hymn,
While ardent Vulcan leaves his home to see
           The Cyclopes at work in factories grim.

Now is the time to crown your shining head
           With heavy leaves from the green myrtle-tree
Or with fresh flowers taken from their bed,
           The flowers which the loosened soils set free.

Now, also, is the time to sacrifice
           In woods that from the sun lie darkly hid
To Faunus, known as Pan, his stated price,
           A lamb or, if he should prefer, a kid.

Pale death with undiscriminating tread
           Knocks at kings' castles and the poor man's inn,
And life's brief sum, o blessed friend soon dead,
           Does not allow us long hopes to begin.

The pressing night will soon upon you come,
  The shades and ghosts that storytellers know,
And Pluto's realm, where exiles have their home;
  And once you thither on your journey go

You'll draw no monarchies of wine by lot,
  Nor stop and stare at Lycidas's charm:
Now he makes all the young men boiling hot,
  And soon the young ladies will grow quite warm!

I.5
To Pyrrha
Quis multa gracilis

Who's the slim boy that hugs you now
  Among the roses, Pyrrha dear,
While flowing perfumes bathe his brow
  Under a pleasant rock somewhere?

Now you tie back your flaxen hair,
  Simple and neat beneath his gaze.
Ah, but in tears he will soon swear
  Faith and the gods have changed their ways.

He will stare out and watch the sea
  Boil at black winds. How raw he is,
Who now enjoys you credulously,
  Trusting your gold, hoping you are his,

There to be loved and open wide
  Always; not knowing the false breeze!
I pity those who have not tried
  Your shining waters. Through with the seas,

My plaque on Neptune's temple wall
  Shows that in dedication I
Have hung my sodden garments all
  In honour of his potency!

I.6
To Agrippa
Scriberis Vario

Your bravery and victories o'er the foe
Let Varius, our Homeric songbird, pen;
Ferocious feats that all the world should know
        Performed on ship and horse by Agrippa's men.

These noble themes I'll not attempt to write,
Nor wily Odysseus' course across the sea,
Dauntless Achilles' stomach for the fight
        And Pelops' house with its foul savagery.

Too slight for such grand things, my sense of shame
And Muse that governs an unwarlike lyre
Bar me from spoiling excellent Caesar's name
        And yours, through praise my talents can't inspire.

Of Meriones black with Trojan dust
Or adamantine Mars dressed for the fight
Or godlike Diomede, Minerva's trust,
        Some poets, perhaps, could with distinction write.

I sing of parties, of young girls who yearn
To fight their boyfriends with trimmed finger-nails.
I can be empty-headed, or can burn.
        Whatever, my wit usually never fails!

I.7
To Plancus
Laudabunt alii claram Rhodon

Others can praise bright Rhodes or Mytilene
        Or Ephesus or Corinth's walls between
Two seas, Thebes (Dionysus' noted city),
        Apollo's Delphi, Thessaly's Tempe pretty;
And some write endless poems to add renown,
        Their life's sole work, to virgin Pallas' town,
Tearing down olive-leaves to bind their brow;
        Many, to honour Juno, will avow
That Argos with its horses is divine
        Or sumptuous Mycenae is more fine.
Enduring Sparta and the open plain
        Of fertile Larissa, no, these again

Have never struck me so much as the home
        Of resonant Albunea or the foam
Of hurtling Anio or Tibur's lush wood
        And orchards where the mobile rivulets flood.
Clear south winds often wipe clouds from dark skies;
        The showers don't last for ever. If you're wise,
Remember to end your sadness: with sweet wine
        Soften life's labours, whether standards shine
Around you in the barracks or you are laid
        Resting amid your own Tibur's dense shade.
Teucer, escaping Salamis, it's said,
        And fleeing from his father, his forehead
Damp from Bacchus, around his temples tied
        A poplar crown; to his sad friends he cried,
"Wherever fortune takes us, it will prove
        Better, my comrades, than a father's love.
Abandon not your hope while Teucer is
        Your leader and observes the auspices:
Unerring Phoebus promised there will stand
        A second Salamis in a new land.
O allies and companions, you have dared
        Much with me and my worst misfortunes shared:
Now turn to wine and drive away your sorrow,
        We'll sail the vast sea once more on the morrow!"

I.8

To Lydia

Lydia, dic, per omnis

Lydia, please tell me this
        Truly by the gods above,
Why do you drive Sybaris
        To destruction with your love?

Now he hates the field of sports,
        Though he once bore dust and sun,
Refuses to ride a horse
        With an armed companion,

Will not break a Gallic mare
        Straining at a sharp-toothed curb,
Yellow Tiber he won't dare
        Touch, and athletes' oils disturb

Him more than a viper's blood;
　　　　Forearms he'll no longer show
Bruised from combat; often he would
　　　　Win first prize at discus throw,

And the javelin he would fling
　　　　Way beyond the boundary line.
Why is he hiding, as, poets sing,
　　　　Once the son of the marine

Thetis, at Troy's tearful end,
　　　　Hid, in case a man's attire
Should before his due time send
　　　　Him to slaughter by Lycian fire?

I.9
To Thaliarchus
Vides ut alta stet nive candidum

Soracte stands before your eyes
White with deep snow, the labouring woods
　　　　Can't hold their burden, and the floods
　　　　Are stilled, set fast with jagged ice.

So come and melt away the cold,
Pile high the logs upon the fire,
　　　　And generously from a Sabine jar
　　　　Draw off a vintage four years old.

The rest leave to the gods: they make
The winds that battle on raging sea
　　　　At once grow calm, and instantly
　　　　Cypress and old ash cease to shake.

Don't ask what will tomorrow bring;
Count every day, that Chance above
　　　　Shall grant, a plus. Shun not sweet love
　　　　Or, while you're young, to dance and sing,

For now you are green, and grey hair sour
Is far off: sports field and the square,
　　　　Smooth whispers in the twilight air
　　　　Should be claimed now, at the appointed hour,

Soft laughter that betrays a girl
Who in some deep nook hides her charms,
　　　　And a pledge stolen from her arms
　　　　Or finger that will just uncurl.

I.10
Hymn to Mercury
Mercuri, facunde nepos Atlantis

O Atlas' grandson, smoothly eloquent,
Primitive men were savage and unkempt:
You moulded us with language and the rule,
    Shrewd Mercury, of the elegant wrestling school.

O messenger of gods and Jove their king,
O father of the curved lyre, I'll sing
Of you and your skill when you hide away
    Whatever you desire in furtive play.

When you removed his oxen by your craft,
Apollo, empty-quivered, stood and laughed.
He scared you, still a child, with threatening cries
    If you did not return his special prize.

Rich Priam escaped the Atrides in their pride
When he left Ilium with you as guide;
He slipped past the watch-fires of Thessaly
    And the encampment of Troy's enemy.

You lay the spirits of the good to rest
Within the settled realms of happiness;
Your gold wand rules the insubstantial host,
    Friend of the highest gods and nethermost.

I.11
To Leuconoe
Tu ne quaesieris

Ask not what term the gods have granted me
    Or granted you,— to know is surely wrong.
Ignore the numbers of astrology
    And do not test the charts of Babylon.

It's better far to suffer what will be,
    Whether Jove has allotted winters more,
Or this, your last, wears out the Etruscan sea
    Against the pumice rocks that stand before.

Be smart, my dear; filter the wine instead.
    Cut back long hope to the brief space you have.
While we talk, envious lifetime will have fled:
    Harvest the day; don't think the future's safe.

I.12
Prayer for Augustus Caesar
Quem virum aut heroa

Which man or which hero deserving of fame
To the sound of the lyre or shrill pipe will you sing,
O Clio? Which god? And whose is the name
    Whose echo will ring

In jest on the shady sides of Helicon,
Or on Pindus' summit or Haemus' mount chill,
Whence thoughtless woods followed Orpheus and the song
    He chanted to still

The fast-falling rivers and swift-rushing winds
With his mother's spell, the Muse Calliope,
As he charmed the attentive oak-trees with his strings
    That sang so sweetly?

But first, with the praise that is customary,
I'll tell of our Father, who guides with his powers
Men's and gods' affairs, and the world, lands and sea,
    With their changing hours.

From him is begotten nothing to compare,
Not like him, or second, or that could surpass;
But the nearest honours are taken by her,
    The goddess Pallas.

Nor will I ignore you, so bold in the fight,
O Liber, and virgin Diana, the foe
Of wild beasts, or, feared for your arrow's sure flight,
    Phoebus Apollo.

I'll tell, too, of Hercules and Leda's sons,
One peerless at boxing, one matchless on horse:
As soon as seafarers spy the refulgence
    Of their pure white stars,

Then down from the rocks the tossed waters soon flow,
The winds fall in concert and all the clouds flee,
The threatening wave, once they've wished it so,
    Lies back in the sea.

I could, after these, first of Romulus sing,
Pompilius' quiet reign, Tarquin's rod and his pride,
Or I could perhaps with great Cato begin,
    How nobly he died.

Regulus, the Scauri and Paulus' abuse
Of his mighty soul when Carthage vanquished us,
I'll gladly recall with Rome's glorious Muse,
    Or Fabricius.

He, Curius too, with his disshevelled head,
And Camillus, also, were made fit for war
By harsh poverty, an ancestral farmstead
    And a suitable Lar.

Like a tree of unknown age, Marcellus's fame
Still grows, and there shines amid Romans all
The Julian star, like a great moon aflame
    Among fires small.

O Father and Guardian of the human race,
Begotten of Saturn, the fates bid you care
For Caesar. May you reign, but in second place
    Augustus Caesar!

Whether he drives off the Parthian hordes,
Their threat against Rome in just triumph subdued,
Or conquers the Chinese from far eastern shores
    Or Indians rude,

Beneath you in justice he'll rule a glad world. –
And you'll shake Olympus with your awesome car;
On impious groves you'll send thunderbolts hurled
    In wrath from afar.

I.13
To Lydia
Cum tu, Lydia, Telephi

When you describe Telephus' charms,
      His rosy neck, his waxen arms,
I become bilious,— ah, well!—
      My liver starts to seethe and swell.

My mind and colour don't stay still
      And furtively a tear will spill
Onto my cheeks and clearly show
      How my heart wastes with fires slow.

I burn when quarrels fuelled by wine
      Have spoiled your shoulders white and fine,
Or if in wild passion the youth
      Has branded your lip with his tooth.

No, if you truly heeded me,
      You would not hope he'd constant be,
Who loves to savage the sweet lips
      Which Venus in her nectar dips.

Thrice happy those, and more than thrice,
      Whom an unbroken love-knot ties:
No harsh word will their true love fray
      Until they reach their dying day.

I.14
To the ship of state
O navis, referent in mare te novi

O ship, once more will the fierce wave
  Take you to sea? Ah, what's to do?
Hold fast to harbour and be brave!
  Your side is bare of oars: don't you
    See this, and how the African blast
    Has left you with a wounded mast?

Your yardarms groan. Without a cable
  Your hull can hardly against a swell
Of such imperiousness keep stable.
  Intact you've not a single sail,
    Nor have you gods with whom to plead
    In this your second time of need.

You may be pine from Black Sea coasts,
  A noble daughter of the trees:
Lineage and name are idle boasts.
  The fearful sailor on the seas
    Trusts not in painted poops. Take stock,
    Unless you want the winds to mock!

Of late you were my deep concern,
  My wearisome anxiety;
Now for your safety I still yearn,
  And this is no slight care for me.
    Avoid the currents of the seas
    Around the shining Cyclades!

I.15
The prophecy of Nereus
Pastor cum traheret per freta navibus

As the herdsman with his Idean navy
Sailed through the straits and, faithless, dragged away
His hostess Helen, mighty Nereus cast
Unwelcome sleep upon the tailwinds fast,
That he might sing the savage fates to come:
"With evil omen do you take her home,
 Whom Greece with many a soldier will recover;
 For Greece has sworn an oath to break your lover
 And you in twain, and Priam's kingdom old.
 Alas, for horses and for warriors bold
 How great the sweat! What piles of death you amass
 For Dardanum! Now the divine Pallas
Prepares her helmet and her bronze attire,
Her chariots and her consuming ire.
Ah, vainly bold, trusting that Venus may
Protect you, you will comb your hair and play
Songs ladies love to hear on the unwarlike lyre,
And vainly to your bedroom you'll retire,
Avoiding dread spears, barbed arrows from Crete,
The battle din and Ajax' fast pursuit,
But in the end, alas, you surely must
Defile well-groomed adultery with dust.
Laertes' son, who marks your people's end,
And Nestor whom the folk of Pylos send,
See you not them? Teucer from Salamis
And Sthenelus, who in close fighting is
So expert, and no idle charioteer
When horses need firm governance, press on near
Undaunted. You will recognise Merion.
See how, in a black fury, Tydeus' son,
His father's better, seeks you out, while you,
As a deer, when a wolf comes into view
On some vale's far side, will its grass forget,–
With high-pitched breaths you'll flee, effeminate.
It was not this you promised to your love!
Achilles' wrathful navy will put off
The day for Phrygian mothers and for Troy;
Their ordained sum of winters they'll enjoy,
But, after that, Achaean flames will come
And burn the homes of Trojan Ilium."

I.16

A lover's apology

O matre pulchra filia pulchrior

O fairer daughter than a mother fair,
Impose whatever sentence you decree
   On my slanderous iambics, whether you care
        To burn them or to throw them in the sea.

Not Dindymene, nor Apollo divine,
The Pythian god who inhabits Delphi,
   So shakes the minds of his priests in their shrine,
        Nor Liber; nor do monks of Cybele

So clash their shrill cymbals, as anger sad
That fears not Serbian sword, nor the event
   Of shipwreck at sea, nor infernos mad,
        Nor Jupiter's tumultuous descent.

Prometheus added to the primal slurry
Under compulsion, so it's said, a part
   Extracted from each creature, and the fury
        Of the insane lion was grafted to our heart.

Anger brought Thyestes ruinously low
And was the final cause for cities tall
   To perish utterly, and the haughty foe
        Turned over with his plough the impressed wall.

Compose your mind: the passion in my breast,–
For I was angry, too, and young and sweet,–
   My raging passion put me to the test
        And made me pen those swift iambic feet

In fury. Now I want sad things to end
And change to gentleness. Oh, now you see
   My cruel taunts' recantation, be my friend;
        Give back your heart and give mine back to me!

I.17
To Tyndaris
Velox amoenum saepe Lucretilem

Swift Faunus often changes his retreat
  On Mount Lycaeus for this lovely hill,
Defending my goats from the fiery heat
  Of summer, and from winds and rainstorms chill.

The nannies roam safely across the estate
  To see where wild thyme and the arbutus hide,
Those wandering wives of a foul-smelling mate.
  They're not afraid of the green serpents' bite,

Nor of the martial wolves which stalk on high,
  As with the sound of the sweet pipes, my friend,
The valleys, and the polished rocks that lie
  In gentle Ustica, echo to their end.

The gods protect me and the gods hold dear
  My piety and my Muse. For you there'll be
An overflowing cornucopia here
  Of glorious rural hospitality.

Here you'll escape in my secluded vale
  The dog-days' heat; the Teian lyre you'll play
And tell of two loves sighing for one male,
  Penelope, and Circe bright as day.

Here too, beneath the shade, you'll sit and pour
  Some glasses of my harmless Lesbian wine,
And drunken Bacchus with Mars will not war;
  You'll fear not impudent Cyrus' design,

For your suspicion is that he will dare
  Lay bold hands on your not-so-weak weakness,
And tear apart the garland in your hair
  And innocently undeserving dress.

I.18
To Varus
Nullam, Vare, sacra vite

Before the sacred vine, my friend, don't plant a single tree
In the soft soil of Tibur and around Catilus' wall,
For truly what god sets before teetotallers is all
Rough fare, and wine alone makes mordant cares disperse and flee.

Who, after wine, bleats of grim service or of poverty?
Who wouldn't rather toast the gods of drinking and true loves?
And yet, so no-one transgresses the bounds Liber approves,
The Centaurs' and the Lapiths' fight to the death over wine must be

A warning,— the Sithonians, whom Euhius afflicts, too,
For they distinguish right from wrong by a too narrow line,
Greedy to sate their lusts. But I'll not vex you, god of wine,
Bright Bassareus, against your will, nor show for all to view

The mysteries of your diverse leaves. Calm the wild drum's excess
And Berecyntian horn, for blind Self-love attends close by,
And Boast that raises up its empty head far, far too high,
And, prodigal with secrets, Trust more transparent than glass.

I.19
Glycera
Mater saeva Cupidinum

Mother of Cupids, Venus wild,
      Bacchus, Theban Semele's child,
Frolicsome Licentiousness,
      All put me under duress
To give back my heart and mind
      To the love I once resigned.

I'm on fire with passion for
      Glycera, whose skin glows so pure,
Parian marble can't impress
      More than her own loveliness.
I burn at her wanton grace
      And her too seductive face.

Venus overwhelms me, quitting
      Cyprus and no talk permitting
Of the Scythians from the Black
      Sea, or Parthian on horseback
Turned in spirited defence,–
      Nothing without relevance.

Bring me fresh turf here, young men;
      Bring me bunches of vervain,
Incense and dishes that hold
      Unmixed wine that's two years old:
Once a victim has been slain,
      Love will come in gentler vein.

I.20
To Maecenas
Vile potabis modicis Sabinum

You'll drink from just an ordinary mug
    A common Sabine wine,
That I once sealed and stored in a Greek jug,
    Distinguished knight of mine,

When, in the theatre, you drew such applause
    Ancestral Tiber's banks
And Vatican's mount, with sportive echoing roars,
    At once returned their thanks.

Grapes tamed by Calenian press, or Caecuban wines,
    Imbibe them if you will:
My cups aren't blended with Falernian vines
    Or those from a Formian hill.

I.21
Hymn to Diana and Apollo
Dianam tenerae dicite virgines

Sing of Diana, sing, young girls;
Sing, boys, of Cynthius with long curls
   And Lato whom our supreme Jove
   Adores with deep, enduring love.

Praise her who joys in streams and woods,
Where leaves o'erhang the icy floods
   Of Algidus, the dark forest scene
   Of Erymanth or Cragos green.

Young men, laud Tempe with like praise
And Delos, Apollo's birthplace,
   His quiver on his shoulder brave,
   And lyre that once his brother gave.

War's tears, famine and pestilence
He'll drive from Romans and Rome's prince
   Augustus to the Persian race
   And Britons, inspired by your prayers.

I.22
To Fuscus
Integer vitae scelerisque purus

The man, whose life is blameless and who goes
Pure of wrongdoing, needs no Moorish spear,
Nor bow, nor quiver pregnant with arrows
    Which on their tips a venomous poison bear,

Whether he makes his journey across the sands
Of seething Syrtes, or the inhospitable
Mountains of Caucasus, or those far lands
    Washed by the Hydaspes renowned in fable.

A wolf came on me in a Sabine wood
While I was singing of my Lalage,
Roaming outside my estate in carefree mood;
    And, though I was unarmed, it fled from me,–

A monster such as Daunia could not rear,
That warrior province with oak-forests wide,
Nor Juba's land produce, Numidia,
    The parched wet-nurse of many a lions' pride.

Set me upon the plains of sluggishness,
Where summer's breeze refreshes not one tree,
Upon the world's edge, where dank mists oppress
    And Jupiter in his malignancy;

Set me beneath the chariot of the sun
That comes too close, in lands which homes deny:
Sweet-laughing Lalage, she'll be the one
    I'll love; I'll love sweet-speaking Lalage.

I.23
To Chloe
Vitas inuleo me similis

You are avoiding me like a young deer
  Who seeks, across the mountainside untrod,
Her anxious mother and, with needless fear,
  Is terrified by breezes and the wood.

Whether the supple leaves, when spring has come,
  Begin to bristle, or green lizards part
The blackberry-bush's brambles in autumn,
  She trembles, shaking in her knees and heart.

But I don't stalk you like a tiger wild
  Or lion of Gaetulia, with a plan
To break you in two: at last it's time, my child,
  To leave your mother and follow a man.

I.24
To Virgil
Quis desiderio sit pudor

Mourning so dear a person, who can have
Proper restraint? Teach us, Melpomene,
Your mournful songs with the voice clear and high,
    Which, with the stringed guitar, your father gave.

So now perpetual sleep presses upon
Quintilius. Restraint, untarnished Faith,–
The sister of Justice,– and naked Truth,
    When will they find the like of such a one?

At his death, Virgil, many good men have wept;
None has wept more than you. Pious in vain,
You ask the gods to bring him back again.
    'Twas not for this that they his credit kept.

Though more seductively you ruled the lyre
Than Orpheus, and trees listened as you played,
Would blood return into an empty shade,
    Which Mercury has once, with rod so dire,

And deaf to prayers which seek the fates to bend,
Compelled to join the dark flock of the night?
'Tis hard, but patience makes the pain more light
    Of that which it is sinful to amend.

I.25
To Lydia
Parcius iunctas quatiunt fenestras

Now impudent youths seldom throw
Their volleys at your closed window;
They don't deprive you of your sleep,
But door is in love with doorstep,

When once it slid on an easy hinge;
Now, less and less, you hear them whinge,
"I'm yours and through the long nights die,
 And, Lydia, do you sleeping lie?"

Instead, you'll weep, a poor old maid,
At fornicators who've betrayed
You, slighted in a lonely alley,
As Thracian winds make Bacchic sally

When the old moon gives way to new.
Then, blazing love, wild passion, too,
Which drives mares crazy, will engage
And round your ulcerous liver rage,

And you'll complain that cheerful boys
Rather in green ivy rejoice
And dark myrtle, and dedicate
Dry leaves to Hebrus, winter's mate.

I.26
For Lamia
Musis amicus tristitiam et metus

I'm a friend of the Muses, so sadness and fear
I'll consign to the violent winds to bear
To the Cretan Sea, and I simply don't care
Which king underneath the Northern Star
Creates some panic on a frozen shore,
Or why Tiridates is struck by terror.

Sweet Muse, who in pure-flowing springs has such fun,
Weave garlands of flowers that bloom in the sun,
And weave my dear Lamia a musical crown.
Without you, my Pimplean Muse, the renown
I confer profits nothing, so let the tune come
With new-fangled strings and a Lesbian plectrum.

May you and your sisters be pleased to consent
To Lamia being honoured with your sacrament.

I.27
The drinking party
Natis in usum laetitiae scyphis

Goblets were made to further man's delight;
It's just the Thracians who use them to fight.
  So give up these barbaric ways of yours,
  Keep modest Bacchus out of bloody brawls.

Lamplight and wine, and a Mede's scimitar,
Are poles apart. How impious you all are!
  Control your shouting, voices down, my friends;
  Keep to your seats, and please control your hands.

Must I drink strong Falernian wine as well?
Megilla's brother from Opus must tell
  What wound it is that makes him so happy,
  And whose arrow it is that makes him die!

You're not keen? I'll drink for no other price.
Your amorous transgressions are so nice
  And well-bred: by whatever love you're tamed,
  You burn with fires that can't make you ashamed!

Whatever you might say, our ears are sure
Repositories. Oh, dear! What a whore!
  A whirlpool! What a workload, what a dame!
  Poor boy, you do deserve a better flame!

What sorceress with drugs from Thessaly
Can free you? What wizard? What god on high?
  Even Pegasus could barely extricate
  You, caught up in Chimaera's triple shape!

I.28
Archytas and the sailor
Te maris et terrae

Archytas, you once measured sea and land
    And the numberless sand;
Now by the Matine shore your slight reward must
    Be a handful of dust
Confining you. To you no good has come
    From exploring heaven's home,
Or running o'er the round arch of the sky
    With a mind doomed to die.
Pelops' father died, and with gods he dined;
    And to the gentle wind
Tithonus was removed, and Minos, too,
    Who Jove's own secrets knew;
Panthoides the depths of Tartarus hold,
    Twice down to Orcus called,
Who, invoking the Trojan age, revealed
    By taking down his shield
That naught except his sinews and his skin
    To dark death had he given,
No mean authority of nature, in your view,
    And of that which is true.
But one night waits for all men, and death's road
    Must once by all be trod.
The Furies present some men in a show
    For grim Mars; sailors go
To meet their end in grasping ocean's waves;
    And so the mingled graves
Of old men and of young are thickly piled, –
No head is spared by Proserpina wild.

I, too, was taken, when the swift south wind,
    Sloping Orion's friend,
O'erwhelmed me in waves of the Illyrian Sea.
    Do not be niggardly
Or grudge a particle of shifting sand
    For my bones, sailor, and
Unburied head: so, when the east-wind raves
    Against the western waves,
Venusian woods be punished, you be spared,
    And may a rich reward,
From every source it can, to you flow down,
    From fair Jove, and Neptune

In whose care sacred Tarentum belongs.
    Will you commit such wrongs
As harm your innocent children after you?
    Perhaps the justice due
And lofty recompense might be your gift.
    No, I would not be left
With my prayers unavenged; no remedy
    Would ever set you free.
Although you hasten, it's no long delay;
Just throw dust down three times, then fast away.

I.29
To Iccius
Icci, beatis nunc Arabum invides

Do you now covet the Arabs' blessed store
 Of treasures, and prepare violent campaigns
Against the Sheban kings, who ne'er before
 Were vanquished, and fashion your woven chains
For the rough Mede? Which of those foreign girls
 Will serve you when her young love has been slain?
Which princely boy with oiled and perfumed curls
 Will be assigned to fill your cup again,
Though he was taught to use his father's bow
 And fire oriental arrows? Who would deny
That rushing torrents can reverse their flow
 On sheer mountains, and Tiber backward fly,
When, in exchange for all the books you amass
 Of great Panaetius and the Academy,
You plan to purchase a Spanish cuirass,
 Though you once promised better things to me?

I.30
Prayer to Venus
O Venus, regina Cnidi Paphique

    Venus, queen of Cnidos, pray,
    Queen of Paphos, come away,
    Your beloved Cyprus spurn.
    Can't you smell the incense burn?
    Glycera bids you fly across
    And visit her lovely house.
    Let your hot boy, Cupid, come,
    Graces with girdles undone,
    Hastening Nymphs, and Youth that is
    Cruel without you, and Hermes.

I.31
Prayer to Apollo
Quid dedicatum poscit Apollinem

What is the bard's behest
  At Apollo's consecration?
  As he pours his new libation,
What is the bard's request?

Not fertile acres of wheat
  From Sardinia's rich soil,
  Not the fine beasts of toil
Reared in Calabria's heat,

Not Indian ivory
  Or gold, not the countryside
  Gnawed by the peaceful tide
Of mute Liris gliding by.

Let those, who such fortune share,
  Prune the Calenian vine;
  Let the rich merchant drink the wine
Bartered with Syrian ware,

And golden cups let him drain,–
  To the very gods he is dear,
  For thrice and four times each year
He sails the Atlantic main

And survives! My favourite food
  Is the fruit of the olive tree,
  The endive or chicory,
And mallows light and good.

Grant, o Latona's son,
  That in good health and, I pray,
  With an unimpaired mind I may
Enjoy the things I have won,

And grant that I do not mar
  Old age with dishonour, I pray,
  And let me continue to play
On the strings of my guitar.

I.32
To the lyre
Poscimur. si quid vacui sub umbra

We're called. If ever, sitting in the shade,
  I've strummed a tune with you that, both this year
And in the years to come, will still be played,
  Come sing a Latin song, o Grecian lyre.

First, by a Lesbian citizen you were tuned,
  Who fought ferociously in time of war,
But, in the lull of arms or having bound
  His storm-tossed vessel on the wet sea-shore,

Of Liber and the Muses he would sing,
  Of Venus and the small boy at her side
Who to his mother constantly would cling,
  And handsome Lycus, black-haired and black-eyed.

O Phoebus' ornament, which Jove on high
  Welcomes at his banquets, fair tortoiseshell,
Solace of labours and sweet remedy,
  Whenever I invoke you, treat me well.

I.33
To Tibullus
Albi, ne doleas plus nimio memor

Don't ache too much in memory
Of Glycera's cruel savagery
Or pitiful couplets rehearse,
Singing your elegiac verse,
Of why faith has been broken and
You're outshone by a younger man.
Lycoris, with her narrow brow,
Is passionate for Cyrus now,
But Cyrus turns his thoughts away
Towards abrasive Pholoe,
And yet a wild goat sooner might
With an Apulian wolf unite
Than Pholoe would sin and be
Found in base adultery.
This is one of Venus' designs,
Who, taking unlike forms and minds,
Sends them beneath her brazen yoke
As part of a barbaric joke.

Although I was loved by a better,
Myrtale bound me with a fetter,
Agreeable to me indeed,
But she's a slave who has been freed,
Fiercer than Adriatic waves
That bend the curved Calabrian bays.

I.34
On the divine
Parcus deorum cultor et infrequens

I seldom took the gods too seriously,
I practised senseless wisdom and I strayed:
Now I must set sail back again, and try
Retrace the abandoned courses I once made.
Jove, who with flashing fire oft parts the clouds,
Through a clear sky his thundering steeds has taken
And winged car, at which the wandering floods
And ponderous earth and river Styx are shaken,
And hateful Hell's cruel halls and Atlas' bounds.
God has the power to change lowest for high,
The great man of distinction he confounds,
He gives bright prominence to obscurity.
  From one man whistling Fortune steals the crest
  And laughs when by another it's possessed.

I.35
To the goddess Fortune
O diva, gratum quae regis Antium

O divine goddess of fair Antium,
  Yours is the power to raise our mortal bones
From off the stepladder's most humble rung,
  Or turn proud triumphs into funeral stones.

You are sollicited in anxious prayer
  By the poor tiller of the countryside
And, mistress of the deep, by whosoe'er
  Stirs with Bithynian keel the Carpathian tide.

The rough Dacian, the Scythian who flees,
  Cities and peoples and fierce Latium,
Mothers of kings in foreign monarchies
  And crimsoned tyrants fear that you will come

And, with the foot of lawlessness, kick down
  The erect column, and that the throng will bray,
Inciting all the laggards of the town
  "To arms, to arms," and shatter empire's sway.

Your slave, Necessity, strides on before,
  With spikes men use for roof-beam fastenings,
And wedges brandished in her brazen claw;
  A dreadful hook and molten lead she brings.

Rare Faith, veiled in plain raiment of pure white,
  And Hope attend you, and as comrades come
Whenever you change clothing and, through spite,
  Choose to abandon a once-powerful home.

But then the faithless mob and perjured whore
  Draw back, and when the wine-jars are drained dry
Down to the dregs, false friends gather no more,
  Too treacherous to share adversity.

Save Caesar, who to the world's end departs
  Against the Britons! Save our hive's new swarm
Of young men, to be feared in eastern parts
  And all around the Red Sea's waters warm.

Shame on our scars, our crimes, our brothers slain!
  Alas, our generation's hardened band
Has shrunk from nothing. We have left a stain
  Of universal wickedness. Youth's hand

Has stopped at nought in fear of gods on high,
  Has spared no altar. Fortune, would you could
Against the Arabs and Massagetae
  Reforge on anvils new our blunted sword.

I.36
To Numida
Et ture et fidibus iuvat

With lyre and incense I'll fulfil my vow
  And, with a calf's blood, gladly will appease
The guardian gods of Numida, who now
  Returns home safe from the far western seas.

To his dear friends he shares out many a kiss,
  But none has more than Lamia sublime,
Who was his king in boyhood's busy bliss
  And donned a man's toga at the same time.

Let's mark with Cretan chalk this glorious day
  And let there be no limit to the wine
From the open jar, and, in the Salian way,
  Let's give our feet no rest from dance divine.

Now Damalis likes her wine in unmixed doses,
  But must not, with one gulp, drink Bassus silly;
No, at our feast, let's have a mass of roses,
  Long-lasting celery and short-lived lily.

They'll all fix watery eyes on Damalis,
  But Damalis has a new paramour:
She won't be torn from that embrace of his,–
  Indeed, the wanton ivy clings not more.

I.37
The death of Cleopatra
Nunc est bibendum, nunc pede libero

Now is the time to drink and beat
The ground with free and easy feet,
  And deck the cushions of the gods
  With sumptuously presented foods.

It would have been a sin before
To bring wine from the ancestral store,
  When Cleopatra's plans were all
  Mad ruin for the Capitol.

Death to the empire she planned then
With her diseased flock of foul men;
  Wildly, she hoped for each desire,
  Drunk with good fortune's sweet liqueur.

But then her rage far less became,
When from the burning fires there came
  Scarcely one solitary ship
  Delivered safely from its trip.

She flew from Italy, her mind
Distracted with Egyptian wine,
  But Caesar, pressing on his oars,
  Soon drove her back to true terrors,

As though he were a hawk and she
A gentle dove, or hunter he
  Swiftly on Thessaly's snowy plains
  Chasing a hare, to put in chains

Fate's monster. She in nobler mood
Sought her end, nor, as women could,
  Shrank from the sword, nor did she race
  With her fleet to some hiding-place.

She dared with face serene to see
Her fallen palace; then bravely
  Handled her deadly snakes, until
  Her body drank the poison vile.

More fierce when she resolved to die,
Scorning a jailer's cruel galley,
  No humble woman, she never sank
  To grace a proud triumph, stripped of rank.

I.38

To a slave boy

Persicos odi, puer, apparatus

I loathe all lavish Persian decoration,
  Dislike crowns that with linden-bark are bound;
My boy, don't bother seeking the location
  Where the late-lingering rose is to be found.

I beg you, please, add no elaboration
  To simple myrtle: for you, serving the wine,
Myrtle is no indecent decoration,
  Or for me, drinking under the thick vine.

Book II

II.1
To Asinius Pollio
Motum ex Metello consule civicum

The civil strife which in the bygone days
  Of consul Metellus began to stir,
The causes of the war, its faults and ways,
  The game of Fortune and our leaders' dire

Alliances, arms stained with unpurged blood,
  You treat, a work that's hazardous and rash,
And so you start your journey on a road
  Across fires lurking beneath treacherous ash.

Now let the Muse of solemn tragedy
  Depart the theatre for a month or two;
Soon, when you have set out our history,
  You'll play great roles again on Cecrops' shoe.

You were the sad defendants' eminent guard
  And of the Senate's high deliberations,
To whom your laurel brought eternal reward
  On your great triumph over the Dalmatians.

Again, now, with the cornet's loud menace,
  You stun our ears; again the clarion roars;
The flash of arms strikes fear in the knight's face
  And terrifies the swiftly-fleeing horse.

Again I seem to hear those generals great,
  Their limbs with not inglorious dust defiled,
And the whole world submitting to defeat,
  Save Cato's spirit that refused to yield.

Once, Juno and the gods of Africa's shores
  Left their land unavenged in impotence;
They brought back grandsons of the conquerors,
  To slay them as Jugurtha's recompense.

What plain is not enriched with Latin blood,
  Where graves the cost of impious wars attest,
The sound of ruin which the Parthians heard,
  Of Italy collapsing in the west?

Which whirlpool and which river have not we
  Made witness to the woefulness of war?
Rome's corpses have discoloured every sea
  And Roman blood is there on every shore.

Abandon not your jests, my wayward Muse,
  Do not in Cean dirges take your fill;
Join me in Venus' grotto, and then choose
  Some music that demands a lighter quill.

II.2

To Sallustius Crispus

Nullus argento color est avaris

Sallustius Crispus, no colour imbues
The silver hidden in the miserly earth:
You treat your coins as though they'd have no worth,
    Unless they shone with reasonable use.

For generations Proculeius' name
Will live; he gave brothers a father's care.
He will be borne on wings, which will not dare
    To be unfastened, by enduring Fame.

You'd rule more widely if you tamed your greed,
Than if you joined Libya with far Cadiz,
And Carthaginians on the two sides
    Submitted to what you alone decreed.

Through self-indulgence dreaded dropsy grows
And thirst is not quenched till the origins
Of the disease have run out through the veins
    And listlessness from the white body flows.

Virtue, dissenting from the common herds,
Returns Phraates to the Parthian throne,
Though of the blessed she numbers him not one,
    And Virtue teaches men to avoid false words.

Her kingdom and sure diadem she grants
To one alone, with her own laurel wreath,
Whoever looks on massive piles of wealth
    But passes on without a backward glance.

II.3
To Dellius
Aequam memento rebus in arduis

Keep a cool head when things are hard,
  In good times curb excessive gladness,
For death will be your last reward,
  Whether you live a life of sadness

Or, lying in some distant grass,
  You sip your best Falernian wine
And toast the holidays that pass.
  The poplar white and the great pine

Form love's alliance, and so marry
  Boughs to cover shady arbours;
The shimmering brook must never tarry,
  As by the slanting bank it labours.

Here send for wines and perfumes sweet,
  The flowers of the rose soon dead,
While age and circumstance permit
  And the three Fates spin out their thread.

You'll leave the woodlands you did buy,
  Your home, the farm yellow Tiber laps;
The riches you have piled up high
  Your heir will drink. Though rich, perhaps,

And born of Inachus' ancient line,
  Or poor and of the meanest caste
Of men under the heavens divine,
  No matter: you will go at last,

A victim by cruel Orcus taken.
  We are all forced to the same fate;
The destiny of all is shaken
  In fortune's cup, sooner or late:
        Into eternal exile we
        Shall go, on board the last ferry.

II.4
To Xanthias of Phocis
Ne sit ancillae tibi amor pudori

You love a slavegirl: do not be ashamed!
Briseis was a slave, Achilles famed
For arrogance, and yet she could excite
   His love with her complexion of snow-white.

Captive Tecmessa's beauty overawed
The son of Telemon, Ajax her lord;
Atrides at his victory parade
   Burned for Cassandra, seized while yet a maid,

After the Asian squadrons and their horse
Fell to Thessalian victors, and the loss
Of Hector gave the weary troops of Greece
   A Troy that could be razed with greater ease.

Perhaps the parents of blond Phyllis are
So rich, you'd gain status as son-in-law;
Ah, doubtless she bemoans her royal blood
   And the injustice of her household's god!

You can be sure the splendid girl you love
Is not from the low classes, and will prove
So trustworthy and so averse to gain,
   Her mother could not ever cause you shame.

Her arms, her face, her rounded calves I must
Wholly commend; and please do not mistrust
A man whose hastening seasons have now made
   Him close the door upon his fourth decade.

II.5
To Lalage's admirer
Nondum subacta ferre iugum valet

Too weak to bear the yoke with subdued neck
  Or meet the obligations of a mate,
When the bull charges in, ready to take
  Love's pleasure, she cannot endure his weight.

On lush green pastures run your heifer's thoughts,
  Cooling the sun's fierce heat where rivers flow,
Or with young bull-calves enjoying some sports
  Amid a moist plantation of willow,

Her favourite pastime. So give up your passion
  For the unripe grape: autumn will come for you
And blue-black clusters elegantly fashion,
  Bedecked with colours of deep crimson hue.

Soon, she'll pursue you. Age runs savagely
  Apace, and will tag onto her each year
That it subtracts from you. Soon, Lalage,
  Seeking a husband, will pertly appear.

She'll be more loved than fleeting Pholoe,
  Or Chloris with her shoulder gleaming white
As the pure moon, which shimmers o'er the sea,
  Reflected in the waters of the night,

Or Gyges! If he joined a chorus line
  Of girls, the obscure distinction would amaze:
Sage guests would be completely taken in
  By his long hair and indeterminate face.

II.6
To Septimius
Septimi, Gadis aditure mecum

You plan to travel with me to Cadiz,
To Cantabrians who've not been taught to brave
Our yoke, and to the barbarous Syrtes
     Where seethes incessantly the Moorish wave.

May Tibur, which an Argive settler founded,
Be home, I pray, for my advancing age.
By Tibur's limits may my paths be bounded,
     Weary of roads and war and sea voyage.

But if I'm kept away by hostile Fates,
I'll seek Galaesus' river, sweet and cool,
Where sheep go out in leather overcoats,
     And fields Spartan Phalanthus used to rule.

That corner of the world smiles upon me
More than all other places where men live.
Mount Hymettus has no sweeter honey,
     Nor green Venafrum a better olive.

There, Jupiter supplies long-lasting springs
And mild, warm winters; there, Mount Aulon's slopes
Give fertile Bacchus friendly offerings
     And are not jealous of Falernian grapes.

That fair location summons me and you
Together; us those blessed heights demand.
There, you will sprinkle with the tear that's due
     The glowing ashes of this poet, your friend.

II.7
To Pompeius Varus
O saepe mecum tempus in ultimum

Into the hour of death you often came
  With me, when Brutus led our soldiery:
Who has restored you to a citizen's name,
  Our national gods and sky of Italy,

Pompeius, first of my comrades-in-arms?
  With you I often wore away with wine
The laggard day, and spread sweet Syrian balms
  Over my crowned locks to make them shine.

With you I felt Philippi and swift flight,
  Ingloriously leaving my small shield,
When manliness was shattered, and the might
  Of youth fell chin-first on the shameful field.

Swift Mercury lifted me through the foe;
  In a thick mist my fearful frame he hid.
But back into the war you had to go,
  Sucked by the currents and the seething tide.

So give to Jove the banquet which you owe,
  Beneath my laurel rest your weary side
Exhausted from your long campaign, and no,
  Spare not the wine-jars that I've set aside.

Fill up the polished goblets to the brim
  With Massic wine that brings forgetfulness;
Pour out sweet unguents from the generous rim
  Of shell-shaped dishes. Quick, who's going to dress

Our crowns with myrtle and moist celery?
  Whom will the dice name Master of the Wine?
I'll outdo the Edonians' revelry:
  My friend is back, I want to lose my mind.

II.8
To Barine
Ulla si iuris tibi peierati

If any punishment for broken faith
  Had ever brought you injury or distress,
If ever you were marred by a black tooth
  Or just one fingernail's slight ugliness,

I would believe you. But, as soon as you
  Have bound with all those vows your faithless head,
You shine more brightly with a beauty new
  And young men ogle at your promenade.

Falsely you swear by your dead mother's urn
  And enclosed ashes, by the entire sky
And stars of night and planets taciturn,
  And by the gods who icy death defy.

I say that even Venus laughs at this,
  The innocent Nymphs laugh and wild Cupid, too,
Who on his bloodstained whetstone sharpens his
  Burning hot arrows ever and anew.

Add this: a whole new generation grows
  To manhood for you, a new band of slaves;
And, though they threaten to leave you, your old beaux
  Still court a mistress who vilely behaves.

At you mothers of young bulls are in dread,
  And mean old men, who cling to their pennies,
And weeping brides, new to a husband's bed,
  In case their grooms are held back by your breeze.

II.9
To Valgius Rufus
Non semper imbres nubibus hispidos

No, not for ever does the piercing rain
Pour from the clouds onto the fields below,
  Nor do the turbulent tempests always blow,
      Tossing the surface of the Caspian main.

In Armenia the still ice does not last,
Or oak-woods groan in high Apulia
  Beneath the north-wind twelve months in the year,
      And ash-trees mourn the foliage that has passed.

But you, with tearful odes, still dwell upon
Your lost Myrtes; your love does not retire,
  Not at the rising of the evening star
      Or as it flees the swift approach of sun.

Nestor, whose life through three generations went,
Mourned not Antilochus for all those years,
  And beardless Troilus' parents shed not tears,
      Nor did his Phrygian sisters all lament

For ever. It is time at last to cease
From your effeminate weeping and wailing,
  And let us rather the new trophies sing
      Of Augustus and icebound Niphates,

How, added to the nations that now yield,
The Parthian river rolls smaller whirlpools,
  And how Gelonians, kept within strict rules,
      Now ride their horses on a narrow field.

II.10
To Licinius

Rectius vives, Licini, neque altum

Your life would be in better shape,
  If you stopped pressing out to sea,
Or clinging too close to the rocky cape
  While eyeing storms so warily.

He, who adopts the golden mean,
  Is safe to avoid a squalid place
With a rotting roof, and isn't seen
  Courting envy in a grand palace.

The giant pine shakes most in the winds;
  The highest towers with the heaviest crash
Fall to the ground; the thunderstorm finds
  The topmost peaks with its lightning flash.

A heart, that's taught to anticipate,
  In bad times hopes, in good will fear
The advent of the contrary fate.
  Jove, who brings back the winters drear,

Also dispels them. Today's bad news
  Won't last for ever. Apollo
Oft with his lyre stirs a silent Muse;
  He doesn't always bend his bow.

When things are tight, be sure you're seen
  Spirited and brave; and, if you're shrewd,
You'll draw your swollen sails back in,
  Whenever the following wind's too good.

II.11
To Quinctius Hirpinus
Quid bellicosus Cantaber et Scythes

What the warlike Cantabrians may conspire
  And Scythians over the Adriatic Sea,
Do not make it your purpose to enquire,
  And put aside all your anxiety

For life's requirements, when life's wants are slight:
  Smooth-visaged youth and gracefulness retreat,
While, grey and withered, old age puts to flight
  The frolics of young love and easy sleep.

The beauty of spring flowers does not remain,
  And the moon's face does not shine only red:
Why raise eternal questions once again
  And with them weary your inadequate head?

Beneath a lofty plane-tree or this pine
  Why don't we, while we may, lie careless here,
And with grey hair rose-scented drink our wine
  And wallow in balm from Assyria?

Bacchus will soon dispel consuming care:
  We need a boy who's able to run fast
With goblets of Falernian wine on fire,
  To quench them in the fresh stream flowing past.

And who will go and lure out that shy tart,
  Lyde, from home? Go, tell her: no delay,
But bring her ivory lyre to play her part,
  Her hair tied in a knot, the Spartan way.

II.12

To Maecenas

Nolis longa ferae bella Numantiae

The long and fierce Numantian war,
Rough Hannibal and Punic blood
Reddening the sea of Sicily should
      Not be themes for a soft guitar.

Fierce Lapiths, Hylaeus drunk with wine,
Earth's children tamed by Hercules' might,
Whose exploits shook the shining-bright
      House of old Saturn divine,

No, not such themes; but one should write
A prose account of Caesar's feats
And menacing kings led through the streets
      Hauled by the neck: that would be right.

My Muse has asked that I should tell
Of sweet-singing Licymnia,
A mistress' eyes that shine so clear,
      A true heart for love shared so well.

How neatly she can dance, and play
Her jokes and games, and throw her arms
Round girls glowing with youthful charms
      On thronged Diana's holiday.

The riches of Achaemenes
Or Mygdon from fat Phrygia,
Would you exchange for just one hair?
      Or the Arabs' opulent palaces,

When she can bend her neck toward
Your burning kisses, or deny
Her love with easy cruelty?
      Licymnia has always adored
        To have her kisses snatched with feeling,
        But sometimes likes to do the stealing.

II.13
To a tree
Ille et nefasto te posuit die

Whoever planted you there first,
It was a day that was accursed,
And with a sacriligious hand
He raised you, tree, so you would stand
A pest for grandchildren to come,
The village's opprobrium.
I would have thought that he could break
His father's or his mother's neck,
And in his inmost sanctum could
Have spattered a guest's midnight blood;
He dealt in poisons from Colchis
And every other crime that is
Conceived in some or other way,
Planting you, timber of dismay,
To fall, inside my own estate,
On an innocent master's pate.
Those things, from which we should stay far,
We barely watch from hour to hour:
The Punic sailor fears the straits
Of Bosporus, but ignores the fates
That come from somewhere out of sight;
The soldier, arrows and the swift flight
Of Parthian cavalry, and they
The chains and jail of Italy;
But death's power, unforeseen till then,
Has snatched, and will, the tribes of men.
Now, I have virtually seen
The realms of dusky Proserpine,
The judgment seat of Aeacus,
The allotted home of the pious,
And Sappho, who lamenting sings,
While plucking the Aeolian strings,
Of girls from her own island home,
And you, playing with gold plectrum,
Alcaeus, songs with fuller notes
Of hardships men suffer on boats,
The dreadful hardships they endure
In flight from battle and in war.

The shades attend each poet's word
Which ought to be in silence heard,
But, with shoulders tight-packed, the throng
Drinks in more avidly the song
Of fighting, tyrants driven out.
What's there to be surprised about,
When songs on those subjects confound
The monstrous hundred-headed hound,
So that his dull, dark, dog-ears droop,
And poisonous vipers recoup
Their strength, all twisted at their ease
In the hair of the Eumenides?
Prometheus and Pelops' own sire
At the sweet playing of the lyre
Forget their toil, nor does Orion
Arouse the fearful lynx or lion.

II.14

To Postumus

Eheu fugaces, Postume, Postume

Alas, the fleeting years slip by,
  And wrinkles and insistent age
Won't be delayed by piety,–
  Nor death that no man can assuage.

Not if three hundred bulls each day
  You sacrifice, will you placate
Cruel Pluto, whom no tears can sway
  And whose sad waves enclose the great

Geryon, thrice our human girth,
  And Tityos: we must all leave shore,
All who enjoy the fruits of earth,
  Whether we're kings or peasants poor.

What use to escape the wounds of war
  Or raucous breakers on the seas?
What use on autumn days to fear
  The southern wind that brings disease?

We must all see the languid flow
  Of errant Styx and the infamous throng
Of Danaus' daughters, as we go,
  And Sisyphus damned to labours long.

We must leave our house, the land we till,
  Our pleasing wife; of these trees we tend,
None but the hated cypress will
  Follow their brief lord to the end.

A worthier heir will quaff the wine
  That with a hundred keys you stored,
And stain the floor with port too fine
  To be served at a pontiff's board.

II.15
The new landscape
Iam pauca aratro iugera regiae

Soon, regal piles will leave few acres here
  For men to plough; on every side you'll see
Ponds stretching wider than the Lucrine mere,
  And everywhere the celibate plane-tree

Will vanquish the elms; soon, beds of violets and
  The myrtle and the nostrils' plenteous hoard
Will scatter their perfumes across the land,
  Where olive-groves enriched a former lord,

And laurel-trees, with branches cut and trained,
  Will keep away the summer's burning blows.
This was not by our ancestors ordained,
  By Romulus' precepts and unshorn Cato's.

For them, men's private wealth was short and quick,
  The public coffers great; no columned porch
Was marked out with a private ten-foot stick
  To intercept winds from the shady north.

The laws did not allow them to dispense
  With casual turf, but made them give their towns
Enhancements at the treasury's expense
  And decorate gods' temples with new stones.

II.16
To Grosphus
Otium divos rogat in patenti

The sailor caught on the open sea
Asks god for peace, as soon as cloud
Has hidden the moon in a black shroud
     And no stars shine with certainty.

Warring Thrace, furious and bold,
The Mede armed with an ornate quiver,
Seek peace, which gems cannot deliver,
     Nor raiment of purple, nor gold.

No treasure stores nor sheriff high
Can shift the tumults of the mind
Or clear away the cares unkind,
      Which round the panelled ceilings fly.

A man lives well on little, whose
Own father's salt-cellar shines bright
On a poor table, and whose light
      Sleep no fear or vile lust removes.

In our brief life man bravely tries
So many shots; he changes one
Place for lands warmed by another sun;
      The exile from his own self flies.

False Care climbs up bronze battleships,
Clings close behind squadrons of horse;
Swifter than deer she runs her course,
      Than Eurus, who the rainclouds whips.

A heart that's happy for today
Should hate to care for the morrow,
Soothe bitter tastes with laughter slow;
      Nothing is blessed in every way.

Swift death removed Achilles bright,
Tithonus long senility
Made weak, and the hour may offer me
      That which it has to you denied.

A hundred herds around you call,
Sicilian cows moo, and the mare
Whinnies, that pulls your four-horse car;
      Twice dipped in African purple

Are your clothes. Honest Fate allowed
Me a small farm, inspiration slight
From the Greek Muses and the right
      To turn my back on the envious crowd.

II.17

To Maecenas

Cur me querelis exanimas tuis

Why, why, Maecenas, do you drain my spirit
With your complaints? Neither the gods nor I
  Will take pleasure if you are first to die,
    Pillar of my affairs and badge of merit.

Oh, if indeed some premature duress
Takes hold of you, a half of my own heart,
  Why do I then linger, the other part,
    Surviving incomplete and valued less?

That day will end us both. I have declared
No false allegiance: we shall go, shall go
  Wherever you shall lead; and we'll follow
    Our supreme journey, comrades well-prepared.

Not if Chimaera's fiery breath awaits
Or hundred-handed Gyas should re-appear,
  Will they tear me away from you, ever:
    So decree potent Justice and the Fates.

No matter whether Libra looks on me
Or fearsome Scorpio, who at the hour
  Of my birth had a more impetuous power,
    Or Capricorn, king of the western sea,

The two of us have stars that correlate
Incredibly. Your glorious guardian,
  The planet Jupiter, from cursed Saturn
    Snatched you and stayed the wings of flying Fate,

When in the theatre the assembled crowd
Cheered you three times in acclamation glad;
  And I, by a tree-trunk falling on my head,
    Was carried off, had not Faunus allowed

His right hand to alleviate the blow,
Protecting Mercury's friends. So bear in mind
  To offer victims and a votive shrine;
    To sacrifice a humble lamb I'll go.

II.18
The simple life
Non ebur neque aureum

No ivory, no gold panels shine
      Resplendent in a house of mine,
No roof-beams from Hymettus weigh
      On columns hewn in Africa,
No unknown heir of Attalus
      Am I, seizing his royal palace,
For me no ladies of good birth
      Trail yards of purple Spartan cloth,
But good faith and a generous vein
      Of ingenuity are mine.
Though poor, I'm sought by rich men and
      Harass the gods with no demand;
I importune no powerful friend,–
      I'm happy with my Sabine land.
Days are displaced by other days,
      New moons press on to end their phase:
You, to the death, contract for cut
      Marble and your own tomb forget.
You build houses and, where seas roar
      Against Baiae, push out the shore,
Pushing as though the wealth to hand
      Were held back by the bounds of land.
And you are constantly engrossed
      In tearing up the boundary post
On neighbouring fields, and jumping o'er
      A client's fence, greedy for more,–
So man and wife, clutching grubby kids,
      Are driven out with ancestral gods.
No hall more certainly awaits
      A rich heir than the ordained gates
Of grasping Orcus. What's ahead?
      Earth opens equally for the dead,
The pauper and son of a king;
      Orcus' accomplice did not bring
Cunning Prometheus back to the world,
      Seduced by bribes of solid gold.
Death can proud Tantalus confine,
      Imprison Tantalus's line;
Death relieves poor men when they call,
      And when they call not, from their toil.

II.19
Hymn to Bacchus
Bacchum in remotis carmina rupibus

I saw Bacchus on distant crags repeat
His songs—posterity believe me, please!—
 And Nymphs learning the words and melodies,
  And Satyrs with pricked ears and goatish feet.

Oh, my mind quivers with this fresh alarm,
My breast o'erbrims with Bacchus, he fills me
 With turbulent joy. Oh, Liber, let me be,
  Let not your fearful thyrsus do me harm!

I must sing of the untiring Thyiades,
A fountainhead of wine, a flowing stream
 Of milk I'll celebrate, that's rich with cream,
  And honey dripping down the hollow trees.

Of Ariadne, your own blessed bride
Who added lustre to the stars, I sing,
 Of Pentheus' rooftops' merciless shattering,
  And how the Thracian king Lycurgus died.

You bend the rivers and the barbarous sea;
In far-off mountain ranges drunk with wine
 You weave the vipers into knotted twine
  And bind the Bistonids' tresses harmlessly.

When the impious gang of giants went to war
And scaled the heights to reach your father's doors,
 You hurled back Rhoetus with a lion's claws,
  And beat him off with your horrendous jaw.

And yet, since it was said that you were more
Fitted for dancing and for sport and jest,
 For fighting you were thought not quite the best;
  But still you held the stage in peace and war.

Cerberus watched you innocently, complete
With your gold horn. He rubbed his tail along
 Your side with soft strokes; then, with triple tongue,
  He licked your legs and your departing feet.

II.20
Epilogue
Non usitata nec tenui ferar

No, on no frail or ordinary wing
  Shall I be borne aloft through empty space,
A poet of double form, nor shall I cling
  Too long to earth, but rise above the place

Of envy and leave cities far beneath.
  I am of poor men's blood; you call, I go.
Yet, dear Maecenas, I shall not meet death
  Nor be imprisoned by the Stygian flow.

Now on my legs a rough patch of skin gathers;
  Above, I change into a pure white swan,
As on my shoulders appear nascent feathers,
  And on my fingers a smooth coat of down.

More famed than Daedalus' son Icarus,
  I'll be a bird of song and I'll fly forth
To see the shores of groaning Bosporus,
  Moroccan sands, and cold plains of the north.

They'll know me in Colchis, in far Ukraine,
  Rumania, where they try not to disclose
Their fear of Latin troops; learn me in Spain
  By heart, and where the Rhonish river flows.

At such an unreal funeral, let's have
  No dirge or ugly mourning or lament;
No acclamation, please, but at my grave
  Let all superfluous honours be absent.

Book III

III.1
The unholy throng
Odi profanum vulgus et arceo

I loathe the unholy throng and I have barred
  Them entry. Hold your tongues, and no more noise!
For I sing songs that never before were heard
  (A priest of Muses, I) to girls and boys.

Though awesome kings control the flocks they own,
  The kings themselves are ruled by supreme God:
Jove's conquest of the Giants won him renown,
  He moves the universe with but a nod.

One man in broader lines may regulate
  His orchard, one with a finer surname
May stroll downhill to be a candidate
  Upon the Campus, one compete through fame

And character, and one may have a host
  Of clients: impartial Necessity
Draws lots of both the best and nethermost,
  The vast urn shakes names in totality.

For the evil man, who sees a drawn sword raised
  Above his neck, Sicilian banquets are
Unable to bring out their long sweet taste,
  And melodies of birdsong and guitar

Bring no sleep: soft sleep, which comes to the bed
  Of country folk, is never so unkind
To humble homes and river banks in shade,
  Or Tempe's valley fanned by the west-wind.

The man, who only wants what is enough,
  Is not disturbed by the tumultuous sea,
By Arcturus' descent, so wild and rough,
  Or by the rising kid-star's savagery;

No, not by vineyards lashed by beating hail,
  Or a mendacious farm, whose trees reproach
First rain, then constellations that assail
  And parch the fields, then unfair winter's touch.

Meanwhile, the fishes feel the waters shrink
  As piles drive into the deep; a busy band
Of contractors and their employees sink
  Dense rubble for a lord who loathes the land.

But Fear and Menace clamber upwards now
  To the lord's mansion; black Anxiety
Sits on the trireme with the brazen prow
  And behind the horseman as he rides away.

So, if the troubled mind can find no calm
  In Phrygian marble, star-bright purple clothes,
Or in the most expensive Persian balm,
  Or in Falernian vineyards, why suppose

That I would want to build in the latest style
  A hill-top palace with a swanky gate?
Why would I wish to change my Sabine vale
  For riches that were more elaborate?

III.2
"Dulce et decorum"
Angustam amice pauperiem pati

Hardship and poverty let him but bear,
The boy who's been toughened by service for war,–
  Let him learn them and welcome them, then ride and go
    To harry the ferocious Parthian foe;

Let the Parthians quake at this knight and his spear,
Let him live under heaven and dare without fear.
  On the enemy ramparts the queen from on high
    Will gaze, and her daughter the princess will sigh,

As her father, the tyrant, is warring below:
"May this prince of my heart, oh this unseasoned foe,
    Not provoke the fierce lion, which blood-lust and wrath
    Drives on through a chaos of carnage and death."

To die for one's country is glorious and sweet:
Death chases the runaway, however fleet;
  It spares not the youth who is loath to attack,
    But sunders his hams and his cowardly back.

Manliness knows of no sordid retreat, –
But untarnished honours lie bright at its feet,–
  Nor accepts nor resigns any office to please
    The judgment that goes with the popular breeze.

Manliness finds a new road to the sky,
Unlocking a path for men too good to die;
  It shuns common gatherings, the earth's soil that clings,
    And flies to the heaven on vanishing wings.

And yet loyal silence also has its due;
The countryside's secrets are holy. He, who
  Dares publish them, won't stay beneath the same beams
    Or share my canoe with me on Sabine streams.

The Almighty, neglected, is not always sure
To draw a distinction between impure and pure,
  But club-footed Punishment, time after time,
    Catches up with the man who's committed a crime.

III.3
Juno's declaration
Iustum et tenacem propositi virum

The man who is just and clings to his intent,
  No fiery baying of the electorate,
No threatening tyrant's glare will make relent
  From his resolve, not Auster, the unquiet

Adriatic's stormy general, nor e'en
  The mighty hand of thunder-flashing Jove:
Oh, if the shattered firmament fell in
  And ruins rained on him, he would fearless prove.

So, Pollux and the wandering Hercules
  Strove to attain the pinnacles of fire,
Between whom Augustus will lie at ease
  And sip with crimson lips divine nectar.

So, father Bacchus, honouring your deeds,
  Your untrained tigers took the yoke and sped
Aloft with you; so, too, on Mars's steeds
  Quirinus escaped Acheron and fled,

When Juno uttered words none could begrudge
  To the assembled gods:"Ah, Ilium!
How deadly and unchaste has been this judge,
  Who with the alien woman has now come

To turn Troy into dust, its fate ever since
  Laomedon stole from the gods divine
Their promised price. Troy, people, fraudulent prince,
  Condemned to chaste Minerva's care and mine!

No longer does that infamous guest have charms
  For Sparta's adulteress, nor perjured house
Of Priam break the Achaeans and their arms
  By virtue of great Hector and his powers.

The war which our own feuds served to create
  Is settled; so, forthwith, my anger sore
And that grandson of mine, whom I did hate
  And whom Troy's priestess, Rhea Silvia, bore,

I shall resign to Mars. I shall allow
  Him to enter these seats of the luminous sky,
Sip juices of nectar and be inscribed now
  Within the peaceful ranks of gods on high.

So long as there extends the savage main
  Between defeated Ilium and Rome,
Let the exiles choose their happy place to reign;
  So long as cattle trample on Priam's tomb

And Paris's, and the wild beasts unharmed
  Still hide their young cubs, let the Capitol stand
Refulgent, and let Rome, ferociously armed,
  Give vanquished Asians her lawful command.

And may Rome spread her dreaded name afar
  To the world's ends,– where the intermediate strait
Distinguishes Europe from Africa,
  Or swollen Nile waters its fields of wheat.

Gold undiscovered Rome will dare refuse,
  Esteeming more that which the earth conceals,
Rather than force it into human use
  With a right hand that all things sacred steals;

Whatever bound is set upon the world,
  She'll touch it with her might, eager to view
The regions where the Bacchic fires have whirled
  And vapours revel with the rainy dew.

But to the warlike Romans I declare
  The fates with this proviso, not to enjoy
Such piety or faith as to repair
  The rooftops of their own ancestral Troy.

Then, re-born under omens of sad weeping,
  Troy's fortune would repeat her loss of life;
Greek troops victorious would be in my keeping,
  And am I not Jove's sister and his wife?

And if Troy thrice rebuilds a brazen wall
  At Phoebus' instigation, thrice again
Will it be cut down by my Greeks and fall,
  And captive wives will mourn their sons and men."

This topic does not suit the cheerful lyre.
  What is your purpose, wilful Muse? Please finish.
The gods discourses only serve to tire,
  And great themes with poor music you diminish.

III.4
In praise of the Muse
Descende caelo et dic age tibia

Come down from heaven, Calliope,
And on your flute a long tune play.
  Sing with high voice, if you prefer;
    Pluck Phoebus' strings, play his guitar.

Can you all hear sweet madness play
With me? I seem to hear and stray
  Wandering through the hallowed trees
    Filled with fair waters and the breeze.

On the Apulian mount Voltur
Outside my nursemaid Pullia's door,
  Tired from my play, a sleeping child,
    On me fabled ring-doves piled

Fresh leaves, a miracle revealed
To all who dwell in the low weald
  Of Forentum, glades of Bantia
    Or nest of high Acherontia.

Mid deadly snakes and bears I slept
Safely, my infant body kept
  In gathered myrtle and sacred bay,
      And blessed with heavenly bravery.

Muses, I'm yours when I behold
The Sabine heights, Praeneste cold,
  Or if the slopes of Tibur please,
      Or Baiae with her limpid seas.

Dear to your springs and dancing, I
Survived the rout of Philippi,
  The fall of the accursed tree,
      The cape on the Sicilian sea.

With you beside me, I would sail
The straits of Bosporus in a gale,
  And dare to walk the burning sands
      Along Assyria's coastal lands.

Inhospitable Britons I would
Brave, Basques drunk on horse's blood,
  Ukrainians with quivers armed,
      The Scythian river, quite unharmed.

When great Augustus craves an end
Of labours and decides to send
  His weary troops back home on leave,
      You heal him in your Pierian cave.

You give mild counsel and rejoice
When it is given. The impious
  Titans and the Giants' revolt
      Were quelled by the falling thunderbolt

Of him, who tempers windy seas,
Still earth, the sad realms, great cities,–
  One monarch who with even sway
      Rules gods and mortal cavalry.

Those warriors caused Jove great alarms
With their faith in their bristling arms,
  The brothers, too, who tried to drop
      Pelion on dark Olympus' top.

What could Typhoeus or Mimas strong
Or Porphyrion, who threatened wrong,
  Rhoetus or Enceladus do,
      Who tore up trees and boldly threw,

When they rushed at the ringing shield
Of Pallas? Here keen Vulcan held
  His ground, here stood Jove's wife Juno
      And he who'll never unsling his bow,

Apollo (who washes his long hair
In pure dew from Castalia)
  Of Delos, Patara, Lycia's thorn
      And native woods where he was born.

Brute force collapses through its weight:
The gods raise force that's moderate
  To greater force; at the same time,
   They loathe force bent on every crime.

One-hundred-handed Gyas is
A witness to my homilies;
  Diana's tempter, Orion famed,
      By her virgin arrow tamed.

Thrown on her own monsters, Earth
Mourns sons, to whom she gave birth,
  All despatched by thunderbolt
      To the lurid underworld.

The swift fire from Orcus' gate
Cannot eat through Etna's weight,
  Tityos' winged guardian must
      Cleave to his liver for his lust,
      The lover Pirithous remains
      Held fast by three-hundred chains.

III.5
The example of Regulus
Caelo tonantem credidimus Iovem

When Jupiter is thundering in the sky,
  We all believe that he is king above;
Augustus, when Britons and Persians lie
  Beneath his sway, a present god will prove.

Did Crassus' soldiers live to be debased
  By foreign wives? By enemies taken in —
Perverted morals and Senate disgraced!—
  To grow old under arms with their wives' kin?

Did Marsians and Apulians conform
  To Persian rule, forgetting the holy shields,
Their name, eternal Vesta, uniform,
  When Jove was still safe and Rome never yields?

This was what Regulus warned with great foresight;
  To shameful terms he vowed not to succumb,
But demonstrated the contingent blight
  Upon a generation yet to come,

If Rome's young soldiers were not left to die
  Captive, unpitied. "Our standards attached
To Punic shrines I've seen; our weaponry,"
  Said he, "without bloodshed from soldiers snatched.

"I've seen the arms of Roman citizens tied
  Behind the backs that once knew freedom's taste,
And opened gates and tilled fields have I spied,
  Which once by Roman soldiers were laid waste.

"I suppose a soldier, when redeemed for gold,
  Comes back the braver! You would just add cost
To the disgrace. Re-dyeing wool that's old
  Does not restore the colours that are lost;

"Nor is true manliness, when once it's gone,
  Concerned to be replaced in weaker men.
Do deer in thickly-woven nets fight on
  When extricated? He'll be valiant, then,

"Who trusted himself to perfidious foes?
  He'll crush them in the next Punic campaign,
When he once feared death and passively chose
  To allow their bonds his biceps to restrain?

"Since he knew not how life was truly gained,
  He confused peace with war. He brought Rome shame.
And you, great Carthage, greater heights attained
  Upon the infamous ruins of Italy's name!"

It's said that Regulus threw off the embrace
  Of his chaste wife, put his small children by,
As though deprived of rank, set his manly face,
  And turned towards the ground a downcast eye,

Till, with unique advice, he won the day,
  Strength to the tottering Senate he restored,
And, mid his grieving friends, without delay
  To honourable exile went abroad.

Although he knew of all the preparations
  That the barbarian torturer had made,
He pushed aside the throng of his relations
  And populace, who his return delayed,

As if, after a lengthy case in court
  On clients' business, when the suit had come
To its determination, he now sought
  Venafrum's fields or Spartan Tarentum.

III.6
Rome's moral decline
Delicta maiorum immeritus lues

Roman, though guiltless, you must now atone
  For your forefathers' crimes, till you remake
The shrines and temples that are falling down
  And the images polluted with black smoke.

You rule the world by putting the gods first:
  From them is all beginning, theirs each end.
When they have been ignored, the gods have cursed
  Hesperia with foul gifts that we lament.

Twice did Monaeses and Pacorus' bands
  Crush our assaults, which the auguries had scorned,
And twice took spoils of war from Roman hands,
  And with them their mean necklaces adorned.

When we were in the grip of civil war,
  Our Ethiopian and Dacian foes
All but sacked Rome, — the one a source of fear
  At sea, the one with volleys of arrows.

That century, fruitful and fat with sin,
  First soiled our marriages, then homes and race;
From this fount devastation flooded in
  Onto our fatherland and populace.

The ripe young virgin thrills now, as she learns
  Ionian dance, and with an artist's skills
Fashions herself; for unchaste loves she yearns,
  When she still has a baby's fingernails.

And soon she looks out for adulterous boys,
  While her own husband in his wines delights;
She doesn't choose who'll snatch forbidden joys
  As her gift when the slaves remove the lights,

But there, before her husband's knowing eyes,
  She rises at the call of the entrepreneur
Or Spanish sea-captain: they buy their prize,
  And pay good prices to dishonour her.

Not from these parents were the young offspring
  Who stained the sea with Carthaginian blood
And struck down Pyrrhus and the mighty king
  Antiochus, and Hannibal the dread.

No, they were rustic soldiers' manly stock,
  Who used the Sabine hoe to turn the soil
And from strict mothers their instructions took
  To cut down timber and to bear the toil

Of carrying logs, as the declining sun
  Altered the mountain shades and brought the hour
For yoke to be released from tired oxen,–
  The happy hour! – with his departing car.

Time's ravages diminish everything.
  Worse than their forebears' was our fathers' age;
We are more wicked, and we shall soon bring
  A more defective future heritage.

III.7

To Asterie

Quid fles, Asterie, quem tibi candidi

Why do you weep? The fair west wind
Will restore your love in the early spring;
  Piles of exotic ware he'll bring,
      Unbroken faith and a constant mind.

The south wind took him to Oricum:
First came the autumn's mad goat-star;
  Now, sleepless, he sheds many a tear,
      For winter's freezing nights have come.

An anxious hostess's messenger:
"Chloe's sad and sighs and burns," he says
  (With fires like yours!); in a thousand ways
      He tempts him craftily to her.

He tells of a false wife's slanderous lie
Driving credulous Proteus on,
  And all-too-chaste Bellerophon
      Despatched by him in haste to die,

And Peleus, almost carried in
To Tartarus, when he chose to flee
  Rather than touch Hippolyte,
      And false tales that teach men to sin.

His lies are vain. Your love, at his voice,
Is deafer than rocks in the sea, and pure...
  Until now. But you must be sure
      To resist your neighbour Enipeus.

There's no-one else who rides a horse
So stunningly on the field of Mars,
  And no-one else who swims so fast
      Along the Tuscan river's course.

Lock your house at dusk, and don't look down
To the street at the song of the querulous flute,
  And though he may often call you rude,
      Just keep responding with a frown.

III.8
To Maecenas

Martiis caelebs quid agam Kalendis

What am I doing, you ask, a bachelor
On this the first of March? What are they for,
The flowers, the box of incense, and the coal
      Piled up on a grass altar? You, the soul

Of scholarship in Latin and Greek lore!
I promised a sweet banquet, and a pure
White kid to Liber, when I was nearly
      Knocked down and buried by the falling tree.

Today's a happy anniversary, which
Will draw a cork, that has been sealed with pitch,
From an old wine-jar ageing by the grate
      Since Lucius Volcacius' consulate.

So take a hundred ladlesful, please do,
To celebrate your own dear friend's rescue;
Light up the lanterns till the light of day, –
      Let noise and anger both be far away.

Don't let the cares of state enter your head:
The troops of Dacian Cotiso are dead,
And Parthian from Parthian dissents
      All waging war with dismal armaments.

Our old Cantabrian foe from shores of Spain
Is tamed in servitude with a late chain;
The Scythians unstring their curved bow
      And now they plan to leave the plains and go.

Relax! A private citizen should not care
Too much what burdens the nation may bear.
Enjoy the glad gifts of this festive tide,
      And put your serious worries to one side.

III.9
The poet and Lydia
Donec gratus eram tibi

He: "As long as I was your delight
          And there was no more potent youth to fling
     His arms around your neck so white,
          I lived more blessed than a Persian king."

She: "As long as for none else you burned
          And Lydia was not Chloe's inferior,
     Though many other heads I turned,
          I lived more glorious than Rome's Ilia."

He: "I'm ruled now by Thracian Chloe,
          Skilled in sweet music, good at the guitar:
     For her I'd not be afraid to die,
          If only fate would grant more years to her."

She: "We blaze with mutual torches, I
          And Calais, the boy from Thurium:
     For him I'd willingly twice die,
          If only fate would grant more years to him."

He: "What if our old Venus returned
          And bound with a bronze yoke two she'd split before;
     If flaxen-haired Chloe were spurned,
          And jilted Lydia found an open door?"

She: "Though he's more beautiful than a star,
          And you lighter than cork, and more angry
     Than the rough sea of Hadria,
          With you I'd love to live and gladly die."

III.10
To Lyce

Extremum Tanain si biberes, Lyce

If you drank from the distant Tanais
  And had married a savage, still you'd cry
To see me battered by the indigenous
  North-wind, as I lay in your rough alley.

Can you not hear how noisily your door
  And spinney, which between fair rooftops grows,
Groan at the bellowing wind, as Jupiter
  With pure divinity freezes the snows?

This haughtiness, which Venus hates, eschew,
  Lest on the wheel the rope should backward fly;
You're no Penelope that none can woo,
  Or daughter of Etrurian gentry.

Although you bend neither to gift nor prayer,
  Nor lovers' pallor with its violet hue,
Nor at your smitten husband's love affair
  With a Thessalian, spare your suppliants, do,

Though you're less pliant than a rigid oak,
  Your heart less gentle than a Moorish snake.
No, not for ever will the heavens soak
  My suffering bones, which on your doorstep ache.

III.11
To Mercury and the lyre

Mercuri, nam te docilis magistro

Mercury, who once in Amphion found
An apt pupil who moved the stones with song;
And Tortoiseshell, you who have practised long
    With seven strings to make your tunes resound,

Though silent once and glum, yet now so dear
To temples and the tables of the rich:
Tell us the measures and music, to which
    Lyde must now apply her obdurate ear,

112

For she's a filly, a young three-year-old
Cavorting on the plain, an innocent
Fearing man's touch and nuptial blandishment,
　　Still unripe for a hot husband to hold.

You can lead tigers and attendant trees,
And stay the course of rivers as they race;
The monstrous gatekeeper of the palace
　　Has yielded to your charming melodies,–

Dread Cerberus, – although a hundred snakes
Defend his head, which the fierce Furies know,
And noxious breath and foul gore ooze and flow,
　　As from his mouth his triple tongue he takes.

Once, even Ixion and Tityos
Gave an unwilling smile, and the urn stood dry
A short while, when your welcome lullaby
　　Delighted the daughters of Danaus.

Let Lyde hear the crimes of those young maids,
Their famous punishment, the empty vase
With water disappearing at the base,
　　And the late Fates, who, even among the shades,

For culpable offences lie in wait.
Those impious girls, what could they do more vile?
Those impious girls drew weapons of hard steel,
　　The murder of their grooms to perpetrate.

One out of many, worthy of marriage
And honouring its flame by perjury,
Addressed her father with a splendid lie,
　　A noble maid for every future age.

To her young husband, "Rise," she said, "and leave!
"Arise, in case the long sleep you yearn for,
Comes from an unfeared source. Your father-in-law
　　And my foul sisters you must now deceive.

"Like lionesses lighting on bull-calves,
Alas, they mutilate them one by one!
I am more gentle. I'll not strike you down
　　Or keep you prisoner behind these bars.

"Let father weigh me down with his cruel chains
For sparing my poor spouse with clemency,
Let him command his fleet to banish me
    To far Numidia's remotest plains.

"Go where your feet lead and the breezes flee,
  While Night befriends you and the Queen of Love;
Go with fair omens, and an epitaph
    Carve on my tomb in memory of me."

III.12
To Neobule
Miserarum est neque amori

It is not done
    for poor girls to play
with love, have fun
    washing cares away
while they're drinking
    wine, or pass out
when they're shrinking
    from an uncle's shout.

Winged Cupid
    has been thieving
your wool, stupid,
    and your weaving
and your duty
    to your crafts are gone
through the beauty
    of a superman.

After rubbing down
    he swims the Tiber,
great Bellerophon
    as a rider
he outpaces;
    firm fist, fleet in
running races,
    he's unbeaten.

In the country
         when the herd's hot
and the stags flee
         he's a fine shot;
when a boar's kept
         down in thick brush
he can intercept
         at a fair rush.

III.13
The Bandusian spring
O fons Bandusiae splendidior vitro

Spring of Bandusia, more bright than glass,
Honoured with pure sweet wine and flowers afloat,
  Tomorrow you'll be given a billy-goat,
    His forehead swollen with the earliest press

Of horns which forecast love and war...in vain!
For this offspring of the lascivious herd
  Is destined to spill out his crimson blood
    And dye your ice-cold torrents with its stain.

The blazing Dog-days at their fiercest hour
Can't touch you with their violence; you know how
  To give warm cold to bulls tired from the plough
    And cattle that come wandering from afar.

Of all the noble springs you'll win renown,
When I tell of the oak-tree on your ridge
  Of hollow rocks, and your clear waters, which
    Chatter away as they come tumbling down.

III.14
To the common people of Rome
Herculis ritu modo dictus, o plebs

Like Hercules, Augustus sought the rewards
  Of laurel wreaths which only death can buy,
But Caesar has come back to his own gods,–
  On Spanish shores he won a victory.

His wife, joyful at her unique husband,
  Shall after holy rituals appear;
The sister, too, of our famed leader, and
  The ladies wearing holy bands of prayer,

The mothers of maidens and young men, who
  Have just been saved. You, boys, and girls who wait
In innocence still for a husband true,
  Refrain from words that tempt an evil fate!

Today's in truth a holiday for me,
  This day will drive all my dark worries forth;
I'll fear no strife, I'll not be afraid to die
  A violent death, while Caesar owns the earth.

Go, find unguents, my boy; find crowns for us,
  A wine-jar that recalls the Marsian war,
Or earthen flask that rebel Spartacus
  Amid his many wanderings never saw.

Go, tell Neaera with her voice so gay
  To bind her scented hair in a quick knot;
But, if you find that there is some delay
  Caused by the hateful porter, homeward trot.

Spirits grow gentler as the hair grows white,
  When they once loved quarrels and brawls uncouth;
I could not, during Plancus' consulate,
  Have suffered this, in the hot flush of youth.

III.15
To Chloris
Uxor pauperis Ibyci

You are just a poor man's wife
    Living an immoral life,
Now it's time for you to shirk
    All your infamous hard work.
As you near your dying day,
    You must now retire from play
Among the girls; you must desist
    From blanketing bright stars with mist.
What suits Pholoe well enough
    May on you, my dear, look rough;
It's more proper for your daughter
    To lead young men to the slaughter,
Like a Bacchante in their home
    Roused by a pulsating drum.
Now love's new compulsions bid
    Her frolic like a frisky kid;

Wool from famed Luceria
    Makes you seem superior;
You're not suited by guitars
    Or the rose's crimson flowers,
Or, now you're on your last legs,
    Magnums drunk down to the dregs.

III.16
To Maecenas
Inclusam Danaen turris aenea

For captive Danae a tower of bronze
  And doors of strong oak, and the dismal sight
Of watchful dogs without, had been defence
  Enough from the seducers of the night,

Had not Acrisius, who jailed the maid,
  Been mocked by Jove and Venus for his fear:
If gods were turned into a bribe, they said,
  The journey would be safe, the pathway clear.

Gold loves to travel though the midst of guards
  And break through rocks with more power than the blow
Of thunderbolts. Through love of rich rewards
  The house of the Argive prophet was brought low.

The Macedonian burst through city gates
  And undermined with bribes his rival kings;
And bribes ensnare rough captains of frigates,
  And they become entangled in their strings.

Increasing wealth creates anxiety
  And hunger for still more. I have been right
Not to expose my crest conspicuously,
  Maecenas, glorious and distinguished knight.

The more that each man has himself denied,
  The more he'll have from heaven; naked, I've sought
To cross the lines and flee the wealthy side,
  And reach the camp of those who desire nought,

The lord of a despised estate, more blessed
  Than if I hid within my granary store
All that the tough Apulians could harvest:
  Amid great riches I am richly poor.

A stream of pure water, a modest wood
   And certain faith in my own cornfield are
A happier lot than shining consuls could
   Enjoy, when governing fertile Africa.

I have no honey from Calabrian bees,
   No wine in Laestrygonian jars matures
For me to drink, no sheep grow their thick fleece
   While grazing on my lush Gallic pastures.

Yet cruel poverty is far away
   And, if I wanted more, you'd not refuse.
Reducing my desires, I surely may
   Better extend my tiny revenues,

Than if I added to the Mygdon plains
   Alyattes' kingdom. Those, who look for much,
Lack much: he's happy, who from heaven gains
   A sparing handful of what is enough.

III.17
To Aelius Lamia
Aeli vetusto nobilis ab Lamo

Aelius, after old Lamus nobly named,—
From him, it's said, your forebears proudly claimed
   Their surname, and authentic records show
      That all their later generations flow

From that sole origin, who, many say,
Was first to own the walls of Formiae
   And river Liris swimming to the shores
      Marica loves, a tyrant prince whose force

Was widely known: tomorrow, the woodland
Will be covered in leaves, and the sea strand
   With useless seaweed will be overstrewn
      By a rain-storm, which the east-wind has sent down,

Unless rain's harbinger, the ancient crow
Deceives me. While you can, gather dry wood now:
   Tomorrow, you'll release your staff from work
      And celebrate with mulled wine and roast pork.

III.18
Hymn to Faunus
Faune, Nympharum fugientum amator

Faunus, the Nymphs flee at your love:
  Across my bounds and country fair
Walk soft and, when you onward move,
  Protect the small ones in my care.

A tender kid at the year's end
  Is yours, and wines to overbrim
The deep bowl, which is Venus' friend,
  And the old altar's smoky perfume.

The herd plays in the grassy leas
  On your special December day,
And in the fields the ox takes his ease
  And villagers have a holiday.

Mid fearless lambs the wolf now strays;
  For you leaves from the wild woods fall;
The ditch-digger gives three hurrays
  And stamps upon the hated soil.

III.19
To Telephus
Quantum distet ab Inacho

How many years there are from Inachus
  To Codrus, who was not afraid to die
For his country, the tribe of Aeacus,
  The wars fought under Ilium's sacred sky,

All this you tell. The price of Chian wines,
  And who will warm the water on the flame,
And when I'll lose the chill of the Apennines,
  And who'll be host, none of this can you name.

Now pour a toast for the new moon, young man,
  A toast for midnight, quick! A toast of wine
To Murena the augur! Our cups can
  Be mixed with three full ladles or with nine.

The inspired poet, who loves the uneven Muses,
  Will thrice three ladles in the bowl demand;
For more than three our Grace strictly refuses,
  Dancing with her nude sisters hand in hand.

She fears a quarrel; I like to go mad!
  Why has the pipe of Berecyntia
Ended its blasts? Why is the flute unplayed
  Hanging together with the silent lyre?

I loathe right hands that are ungenerous.
  Scatter the rose petals! Let Lycus hear
Our crazy din and make an old man's fuss,–
  His ill-matched lady, too, our neighbour fair.

Your hair is thick, Telephus, and you glow;
  You're as unsullied as the evening star.
Rhoda's in bloom for you and wants you so;
  I burn with slow love for my Glycera.

III.20
To Pyrrhus
Non vides quanto moveas periclo

Don't you see that a lioness,
Whose cub's disturbed, is dangerous?
A timid huntsman, you'll soon flee
War's hardships, when through a company
Of hostile youths she goes to seek
Nearchus the outstanding Greek.
A mighty contest it will be,
Whether you win the prize or she.

But while swift arrows you unsheathe
And she whets her horrendous teeth,
The innocent umpire of the bout
Has trampled the palm underfoot
(One hears) and the soft wind caresses
His shoulder beneath perfumed tresses,
Like Nireus or fair Ganymede
Snatched from damp Ida's mountainside.

III.21
To a wine-jar

O nata mecum consule Manlio

O sister, born in the same year as I,
Bringing complaints or gay hilarity,
Quarrels or the insanity of love,
Or easy sleep: holy wine-jar, approve
Whatever name you're given to preserve
Your vintage. On a holiday you deserve
To move. Come down! Corvinus wants to pour
Some Massic that's more drowsy and mature.

He won't ignore you. No, he won't be rude,
Though with Socratic dialogues he's imbued.
Even Cato's propriety grew hot
In olden times, when he had drunk a lot.
Yes, to the character that's quite austere
You bring your gentle torment; you lay bare
The wise man's cares and his secret design
For gentle Bacchus, careless god of wine.

You bring back hope to minds that are unsure,
Strength to the anxious, horns to aid the poor,
Who, after you, fear not the angry intent
Of crested kings or soldiers' armament.
Now, Liber and glad Venus will come by,
The Graces will their tardy knots untie,
And living lanterns will prolong your hours
Till Phoebus comes to chase away the stars.

III.22
To Diana

Montium custos nemorumque virgo

Guardian of mountains, virgin of the grove,
    When brides endure the travails of the womb,
Thrice-called you hear their cries, and you remove
    Them from death's grasp; goddess of triple form:

Above my farmhouse let your pine-tree stand,
    And every passing year in joyous mood,
Just as the wild-boar steadies for its planned
    Lunge from the side, I will donate its blood.

III.23
To Phidyle

Caelo supinas si tuleris manus

If you have raised open hands to the sky
  At the moon's birth, and made your gods a vow
With incense and the year's crops, Phidyle
  My country girl, and killed a greedy sow,

The pestilent wind from Africa won't harm
  Your fertile vine, and sterile mildew shall
Not blight the crops, nor will sweet kid or lamb
  Feel the harsh weather in the fruitful fall.

A victim nourished in Algidus' snows
  Between the oak-trees and the tall ilex,
Or one which in the Alban grasses grows,
  Will stretch its neck and stain the pontiffs' axe

In sacrifice: it's not for you to try
  With vast slaughter to tempt small deities,
Whom you already crown with rosemary
  And garlands of delicate myrtle leaves.

An innocent hand, that's to the altar come,
  Needs no rich sacrifice to allay its fault,
But mollifies the unhearing gods of home
  With holy flour and jumping grains of salt.

III.24
Rome's immorality
Intactis opulentior

Though wealthier than the untapped stores
    Of Arabs and rich India's shores,
And though you fill the whole Tuscan sea
    And Adriatic with debris,–
Since dire Necessity can fix
    Her steel spikes to the highest peaks,
From fear you'll not set your mind loose
    Or free your head from death's tight noose.
The Scythians, who on flat plains roam
    While wagons pull their wandering home,
Live better, and the stiff Getae,
    Whose unallotted lands give free
Produce and cereal all can share,
    Though cultivated year to year;
Each in his turn does equal toil
    For one who's finished with the soil.
There, orphaned stepchildren can find
    A mother innocent and kind;
No dowried wife rules husband poor
    Nor trusts a polished paramour,–
Her dowry's the morality
    Her parents gave, the chastity
That fears strange loves and has sure faith:
    To sin is wrong, the price is death.
He, who will end this impious age
    Of carnage and of civil rage,
If he wants statues with the name
    "Father of Cities", may he tame
Our unchecked immorality
    And win fame from posterity.
We loathe pure virtue, in our sin,
    But at its absence we complain.
What is the use of sad lament,
    If guilt's not pruned by punishment?
What has vain legislation done
    When all morality is gone,
If lands that burning fires enclose,
    Latitudes where the north-wind blows,
Or snow grown hard upon the ground
    Can't keep the merchant from his round,

And crafty sailors rule the main,
    And poverty brings great disdain
And makes us all things bear and do,
    And leaves the path of steep virtue?
Let's throw into the Capitol,
    Where massed bands of supporters call,
Or into the nearest ocean hurl
    Our useless gold, each gem and pearl,
The substance of our greatest ill,
    If true repentance we can feel.
All elements of depraved lust
    Must be uprooted; weak minds must
Be moulded with training more tough.
    The freeborn boy, awkward and rough,
Can't ride a horse and hold his mount;
    He's not only afraid to hunt,
He plays expertly, if you please,
    With Greek hoops or illegal dice.
His father's perjury up-ends
    A business partner and his friends,
So he can pile up cash in haste
    For his unworthy heir to waste.
Dishonest riches build and build,
    But shortages are still revealed.

III.25

To Bacchus

Quo me, Bacche, rapis tui

Where do you take me as I rave?
    To which wood am I driven, or cave?
My mind is strange, I move at speed.
    On which high rocks shall I be heard
Telling the stars and gods the story
    Of great Caesar's eternal glory?
I'll tell a new and noted truth
    Untold by any other mouth.
The sleepless Bacchante on the height
    Looks out amazed at snowy-white
Thrace and river Hebrus' flood,
    And Rhodope crossed by foreign foot;
So, too, as I wander, I love
    The river-banks and empty grove.

O king of Naiads, Bacchantes too,
    Who the high ash-trees overthrew,
I'll no mean words or humbly speak,
    Nothing mortal. It's danger sweet,
Bacchus, to follow a god divine,
    One's head wreathed with green shoots of vine.

III.26
Prayer to Venus
Vixi puellis nuper idoneus

Of girls till now I'd never tire,
I fought campaigns not without glory;
  Now I'll hang up my arms, and lyre
    That is exhausted from war's story.

They'll grace these side-walls, that enclose
The left of Venus of the Sea.
  Here, lay bright torches, crowbars, bows
    That stormed the opposed gates so proudly!

O goddess, queen of Cyprus fair,
O queen of Memphis, where no snowy
  Gusts from Sithone fill the air,
    Raise your whip once, and touch proud Chloe.

III.27
To Galatea
Impios parrae recinentis omen

The unholy should go on their way
  To the ill-omened barn-owl's cry,
The pregnant bitch, the tawny-grey
  Wolf that runs down from the high
    Country of Lanuvium,
    And the she-fox great with young.

A slithering snake should, as they ride,
  Break their journey's proposed courses,
Like an arrow from the side,
  Scaring their Gallic coach-horses.
    I'm a providential seer
    For the one for whom I fear:

Before the bird, which prophesies
   The imminence of violent rain,
On her homeward passage flies
   Back towards the stagnant fen,
      I'll pray for the raven's song
      From the coming of the dawn.

May you, wheresoe'er you are,
   Live in true felicity;
Forget me not, Galatea!
   From the left hand of the sky
      May no bird prevent you go,
      Woodpecker or wandering crow.

Do you see setting Orion,
   With what turbulence he shakes?
I know how the Adriatic can
   Darken and what a swell she makes,
      And how Iapyx from the north-west
      Seems fair and will then transgress.

May the wives of our enemies
   And their children feel the blind
Motions of the nascent rise
   Of Auster, the fierce southern wind,
      And the black ocean's roar and crash,
      And coasts that shake beneath the lash.

So, Europa entrusted her side
   Of snowy white to the cunning bull,
And she paled at the teeming tide
   With enormous monsters full;
      Caught up in a fraudulent lie,
      She blanched at her audacity.

She'd worked among the flowers of late
   In meadow-grass, where she could delight
In weaving a garland to dedicate
   To the Nymphs; now, in the glimmering night,
      Only the stars in heaven could she
      See, and the waves upon the sea.

When to the isle of Crete she came,
   A hundred towns within its sway,
"Father!" she cried. "But that's a name
   Your daughter has just given away,
      And filial piety and trust
      All to a raging passion lost!

"I know not whence or whither I came!
  One death alone is a punishment
Too slight for a young virgin's shame!
  Am I awake as I lament
    This foul crime, or, of vices free,
    Does an empty ghost play games with me?–

"A ghost that flies through an ivory gate
  Bringing a dream while I'm asleep!
Ah, which has been the better fate,
  Over long billows of the deep
    To go, or spend those recent hours
    Picking bunches of fresh flowers?

"If I were given the infamous bull,
  So much anger do I feel,
I would dedicate my all
  To mutilate him with the steel
    And smash the horns of one I loved
    So much, but a monster proved.

"Shameless I left my father's house,
  And now shameless I delay
Committing myself to Orcus.
  Oh, if any god can hear me say
    This prayer, how I wish I could
    Wander among the lions, nude!

"Before my soft and rounded cheek
  Yields to emaciation foul,
And before the juices leak
  From this young and tender spoil,
    I wish, while my looks are good,
    I could be the tigers' food!

"My absent father is urging me:
  'Europa, you are worthless trash:
Why do you hesitate to die?
  You can hang from this mountain-ash.
    Use your girdle to good effect:
    Do some damage to your neck!

" 'If you find the cliffs appealing,
  Or the rocks with points of death,
Come, and give yourself with feeling
  To the rapid storm-wind's breath,
    Unless each day you'd rather pluck
    A mistress' spinning as your work,–

" 'Though your blood is of royal line, –
Or belong to a foreign dame
And be a paid concubine!'"
As she lamented, Venus came,
Smiling falsely at her side,
And her son with bow untied.

Soon, when Venus had done with all
Her sport, "You must hold back," said she,
"From anger and a heated brawl,
When at some future time you see
Your detested bull returns
For you to mutilate his horns!

"You don't know how to be the wife
Of invincible Jove. Now you must cease
Your sobbing. You must learn in life
To carry great fortune with ease:
A continent of the world
Will by your own name be called."

III.28
To Lyde
Festo quid potius die

What better could I do on the holiday
Of Neptune? Lyde, bring without delay
My treasured Caecuban! Your strength apply
To assault the ramparts of philosophy!

The noonday sun's decline you can now feel,
Yet, as though winged day were standing still,
You hesitate to pull down the old wine-jar
That since Bibulus' days has been in store.

We'll sing in turn of Neptune of the seas
And the green tresses of the Nereides;
You'll sing of Lato on your curved lyre
And the sharp darts of speedy Cynthia.

At the song's climax, we will Venus praise,
Who owns Cnidos and the shining Cyclades,
And on yoked swans to Paphos loves to fly;
Then Night in a deserved lullaby.

III.29
To Maecenas
Tyrrhena regum progenies, tibi

Son of Etruscan kings of yore,
Smooth wine from flasks I've yet to pour,
  Maecenas, and the rose's flower
       And oil of ben pressed for your hair

Wait at my home. Quick, no delay,
Don't watch damp Tibur, and Aefula
  With sloping fields, and the mountainside
       Of Telegonus the parricide.

Give up tiresome prosperity,
Your mansion climbing to the sky;
  Don't stare at city smoke, and gaze
       At blessed Rome's wealth and noisy ways.

Often, the rich find change welcome;
Within a poor man's tiny home,
  No purple drapes, but tidy fare
       Will smooth away the frown of care.

Andromeda's bright father shows
His secret fire, and mad Leo's
  Constellation and Procyon
       Rage, as the sun brings dry days on.

Tired shepherds with their languid flocks
Seek shade and stream, and the thorny copse
  Of rough Silvan; mute rivers find
       No respite from a wandering wind.

You care what stance will most become
The state; anxious, you fear for Rome
  The plots of feuding Tanais,
       Of Cyrus' realm and the Chinese.

The future's outcome with foresight
God hides in the dark mists of night;
  If mortals fuss more than they may,
       He laughs. Remember, plan today

With a tranquil mind! The rest is borne
As if by a river slipping down
  Its central channel peacefully
      Out into the Etruscan sea;

But then it rolls up polished stones,
Uprooted trees and herds and homes,–
  The mountains and the neighbouring woods
      All rage and shout, as the wild floods

Harass the peaceful streams. He'll be
His own master and live happily,
  Who day to day can say out loud:
      "I've lived! Tomorrow, with black cloud

"Or pure sun let Jove fill the sky;
 He'll not make void what has passed by,
  Reshape or render it undone,
      When once the fleeting hour has gone."

Fortune enjoys her savage work,
And from her strange game doesn't shirk;
  Uncertain honours she'll transmute,–
      To me, then to others she is good.

I praise her when she stays, but if
She flaps her wings, gifts back I give;
  I wrap myself in my own worth
      And, undowried, woo honest dearth.

It's not for me, if the main-mast roars
In an African storm, to have recourse
  To bargains, vows and piteous prayers
      That Cyprian and Tyrian wares

Should not add wealth to the grasping sea:
Safely in a two-oared dinghy
  Through the Aegean hurricanes
      I'll sail by the breezes and the Twins.

III.30
Epilogue
Exegi monumentum aere perennius

I've made a monument to outlast bronze,
Rise higher than the pyramid of a king;
No gnawing rain, no north wind's violence,
Or countless ranks of years and the fleeing
Of time could e'er this monument erase.
I shall not all die: some great part of me
Will escape Death's goddess. With posthumous praise
I'll freshly grow, be renewed constantly,
So long as priest with silent priestess shall
Climb upwards to the Roman Capitol.

I shall be famed where Aufidus' torrents roar
And where waterless Daunus reigned as king
Of rustic folk. Humble, I rose to power,
And I became the first of men to sing
Aeolian odes transposed to Italian verse.
So take a special pride in these deserts;
Grant me the Delphic laurel willingly,
And crown my hair with it, Melpomene.

Book IV

IV.1

To Venus

Intermissa, Venus, diu

Venus, are you resuming war
       After a long peace? I implore,
I am not the same today
       As when good Cinara held sway.
O sweet Cupids' mother wild,
       Don't bend me with your dictates mild,
Hardened after fifty years.
       Answer young men's flattering prayers!
You had better fly at once
       On the wings of purple swans,
And revel at Paullus' home
       Where your fever can consume
A ready heart: for he's well-born,
       Decent, and no taciturn
Framer of legal defences,
       With a hundred competences;
Far and wide the boy will carry
       The banners of your military
And, when he's achieved success
       And mocked at his rival's largesse,
He'll see your marble statue gleams
       By the Alban lake beneath citrus beams.
You'll smell incense, enjoy the lute,
       Hear the Berecyntian flute,
And the pipe will play along
       With a miscellany of song.
Boys and girls there, twice each day,
       Will extol your deity;
Salian style, with pure white feet,
       They'll shake the earth with triple beat.
For me, no lady love or boy
       Or credulous hope of mutual joy,
No drinking bout helps pass the hours,
       Nor crowning my head with fresh flowers.
But why,- oh, Ligurinus, speak!-
       Does a sole tear slip down my cheek,
And my tongue, amid my eloquence,
       Lapse into unseemly silence?
At night in dreams I hold you tight
       Or follow you as you're in flight
Across the field of Mars, or through
       The rolling waters, cruel you!

IV.2
To Iullus Antonius
Pindarum quisquis studet aemulari

Whoever, Iullus, strives to emulate
Pindar, reaches with Daedalus' aid for the sky
On wings of wax, and is doomed to donate
    His name to the glassy sea,

For, as a mountain-river downward flows
When heavy rains have fed it far beyond
Its usual banks, Pindar boils up and grows
    Massive from a mouth profound.

How he deserves Apollo's crown of bay!
In audacious dithyrambic refrain
He rolls down new words and is borne away
    On rhythms no laws constrain.

He sings of gods and kings, and the gods' blood,–
Of one through whom the Centaurs justly came
To meet death's fall, another who subdued
    Fearful Chimaera's flame.

Of horse and boxer coming home once more,
Exalted by the Olympic palm to the skies,
He tells, and gives a prize of greater power
    Than a hundred effigies.

He mourns the youth snatched from his weeping love,
And praises his strength and spirit and spark,
And golden virtues to the stars above,
    Denying Orcus dark.

A mass of air lifts the swan of Dirce
Whenever he climbs up to the high tracts
Of the clouds. I, I am like a Matine bee
    In my ways and my acts,

Who gathers sweet thyme with incessant toil:
I work around the woodlands and along
The slopes of damp Tibur, a creature small,
    Shaping my busy song.

You'll sing, a poet with a more grand plectrum,
Of Caesar, whenever up the Sacred Way
He, dragging the fierce Sygambrians, should come
      Crowned with triumphal bay,

Than whom no greater and no better thing
Have the fates and good gods given to the world,
Nor will they, even at a new coming
      Of the former age of gold;

And you will sing of joyful days in Rome,
And public games for the return, much sought,
Of valiant Augustus to his home,
      And the empty law-court.

Then, if I can utter words fit to hear,
My voice will also bear its own good part:
At Caesar's welcome, "Praise to the sun so fair!"
      I'll sing with cheerful heart.

Not once, but three times, we will shout the words
"Joy! Triumph!" as you go; the whole city
Will cry and we'll burn incense to the gods
      For their generosity.

Ten bulls and ten cows will absolve your vows;
A tender calf, which in the thick grass feeds
Away from its own mother, as it grows,
      Will meet my promised needs.

The curved fires of the crescent moon, which light
At the third rising, will grace its forehead;
Where it is branded, it will be snow-white,
      Elsewhere a tawny red.

IV.3

To Melpomene

Quem tu, Melpomene, semel

He, whom at birth with kindly eye
    You've once looked on, Melpomene,
Will never rise to boxing fame
    Through hard work at an Isthmian game.
No keen horse with Achaean car
    Will give him victory. No war
Will put him on the Capitol stage
    Adorned with Delian foliage
For crushing some king's trumped-up force.
    But streams, which past rich Tibur course,
And woodlands with leaves thick and strong
    Ennoble him with Aeolian song.
O Rome, of cities the princess,
    Now envy's tooth will gnaw me less:
Your children have set me on high
    In their beloved poets' company.
Pierian Muse, you who instill
    Sweet sounds in the gold tortoiseshell,
Who even to the speechless fish
    Will give a swan's voice, if you wish:
This is all due to your bounty,
    That passers-by now point at me,
The minstrel of the Roman lyre.–
    I breathe and please, but you inspire!

IV.4

In praise of Drusus

Qualem ministrum fulminis alitem

Like the winged servant of the thunderbolt,
  Whom Jove made king of the birds' roving breed,
Himself the king of gods, when without fault
  He helped him win the fair-haired Ganymede,

The bird that once youth and the energy
  Of his fathers drove unpractised from the nest,
But winds of spring, sweeping the clouds away,
  Then taught to put new labours to the test,

Though fearful; soon, with spirited attack,
  He dives upon sheep-pens in hostile flight,
Or falls on serpents as they wrestle back,
  Driven on by love of feasting and the fight;

Or like a lion, that his mother shakes
  Off from the rich milk of her tawny side,–
A deer, intent on happy grazing, wakes,
  To perish from a tooth as yet untried;

So, underneath the Alps, as he made war,
  Was Drusus by the Vindelici seen,
Who through their history by custom bore
  Their Amazonian battle-axes keen.

Whence came this custom need not be revealed,–
  To know all things is not right,– but, though long
And far and wide they conquered in the field,
  They were reconquered by strategems young.

They felt the power of sound intelligence
  And talent raised in an auspicious home,
And of Augustus' fatherly presence
  Towards boys who from Nero's stock had come.

The brave are made so by the brave and good.
  Within themselves the colt and young bull prove
Their fathers' courage; the fierce eagle's blood
  Does not produce the weak, unwarlike dove.

How much, Rome, to the Neros' clan you owe,
  River Metaurus, Hasdrubal's defeat,
And that beautiful day bear witness to,
  When Latium's darkness was made to retreat.

In bounteous glory then, day smiled, the first
  Since the African through the towns of Italy,
Like a flame through pine-trees, rode his ride accursed,
  Like Eurus through the waves of Sicily.

Then, Rome's young manhood knew success, and toiled
  And grew, restoring every holy shrine
That impious Carthaginians had despoiled,
  With upright statues of the gods divine.

At length, perfidious Hannibal declared:
  "We're deer, we are the rapacious wolves' prey!
Perversely we pursue, when our reward
  Is rich if we escape and run away.

"This race, which bravely, from the ashes of Troy,
　Brought sacred relics tossed on Tuscan seas,
And carried aged father and small boy
　Across to the Ausonian cities,

"Is like a great oak, pruned by axes hard
　On Algidus abounding with dark leaves:
Through loss, through carnage, from the very sword
　Fresh spirit and resources it receives.

"The Hydra was not sturdier when it grew
　Its shorn limbs to frustrate fierce Hercules.
No greater monster Colchis ever knew,
　Or dragon Echion's city of Thebes.

"Sink them in the deep, they come out more fair!
　Wrestle, and with great credit they rush out
Against their undefeated conqueror,
　And wage wars for their wives to talk about!

"No longer, now, to Carthage shall I send
　Proud messengers. Destroyed are our hopes all,
And our name's destiny has reached its end
　With the destruction of great Hasdrubal."

So Claudian hands have perfect competence;
　Jove's benign presence keeps them safe and sure,
And Claudian intellect and diligence
　Speed them through the emergencies of war.

IV.5

To Augustus Caesar

Divis orte bonis, optime Romulae

Born of the good gods, guardian excellent
Of Romulus' race, and far too long absent:
Within the sacred council you did swear
　　　To Rome's fathers an early return here.

Come back, good prince; give back your land your light!
When, like the springtime, your face has glowed bright
Upon the nation, then more pleasant runs
　　　The day and more intensely shine the suns.

When the south-wind blows, breathing jealously
Across the wastes of the Carpathian sea,
And keeps a young man lingering on the foam
  For more than one year, far from his sweet home,

His mother, with vows, signs and entreaties, prays
And never takes her eyes off the curved bays:
So, Romans, with a faithful longing, yearn
  That Caesar to his country should return.

The ox in safety roams the countryside
Which Ceres feeds, good Fortune at her side;
And sailors across peaceful waters fly,
  And censure is abhorred by honesty.

The pure house is by no defilement stained,
By law and usage tainted sin is tamed,
New babes are praised for being like their parent,
  Crime is suppressed by attendant punishment.

With Caesar unharmed, who could ever fear
Parthians or foes from icy Scythia,
Or broods which the rough German nation bore,
  Or care for fierce Iberia and her war?

Each man in his own hills passes his days
And weds the vine to the unmarried trees;
Thence to his wines he goes home in glad mood,
  Inviting you to his second course as god!

He honours you with fulsome prayer and wine
From his libation bowls, and you, divine,
He mixes with his own divinities,
  Like Greece with Castor and great Hercules.

"Good prince, give Italy a long holiday!"
In the early morning soberly we say,
When day is untouched, and we say it drunk,
  After the sun has beneath the Ocean sunk.

IV.6
Hymn to Apollo
Dive, quem proles Niobea magnae

O god, your vengeance at their massive boast
  Niobe's children felt; to you Tityos fell,
The rapist, and Achilles who almost
  Became the conqueror of Troy's citadel,

The Phthian warrior, greater than them all
  But not your equal, that son of marine
Thetis, although he shook the towers and wall
  Of Ilium with his awesome javelin.

Like a great pine-tree struck by biting steel,
  Or cypress which the north-wind's blast would wreck,
He spread his giant frame and prostrate fell
  And in the Trojan dust he laid his neck.

He'd not have wished to be shut in the horse
  Which feigned Minerva's sacred offering,
Or dupe Trojans in their rash revels' course
  Or Priam's palace, joyful with dancing,

But would have planned sinful vengeance to wreak
  And, while his captives watched, alas, consume
With Grecian flames boys who could not yet speak,
  Even the child within its mother's womb,

Unless the father of the gods had given,–
  Swayed by your voice and by dear Venus' prayers,–
Walls built beneath a more auspicious heaven
  To save Aeneas' race in future years.

Minstrel, teacher of clear-voiced Thalia,
  Washing your hair where river Xanthus flows,
Smooth-faced Apollo, guard from failure
  Our Daunian Camena, Italy's Muse.

Phoebus has given me his inspiration,
  Phoebus the art of song, a poet's name.
O girls, who are the first girls of the nation,
  And boys who come from fathers of fair fame,

Wards of Delos' goddess, whose bow makes fleeting
  Lynxes and antelopes meekly succumb,
Observe the Sapphic metre and the beating
  On my guitar of this, your master's thumb.

Now duly praise Latona's youthful son;
  Praise the Night-shiner with her glowing light,
Who favours crops and makes the steep months run,
  And swiftly rolls them on in downward flight.

When you are wed, you'll say,"For the gods above,
  When the new century brought festive days,
I once performed a hymn which they did love,
  And I was tutored by the bard Horace."

IV.7

To Torquatus

Diffugere nives, redeunt iam gramina campis

The snows have scattered. Now upon the leas
  The grass returns, and leaves upon the trees;
Earth changes seasons and the floods subside;
  Again within their banks the rivers glide.
Now the three Graces and the Nymphs advance
  And venture out unclothed to lead the dance.
The year, and the hour which steals indulgent day,
  Warn to hope not for immortality.
The winter's cold is warmed by the west-wind,
  And spring gives way to summer, which must end
Once fruitful autumn has poured forth its store,
  And then still winter hurries back once more.
The moons in their swift courses soon repair
  The heavens' damage, but when we fall there,
Where pious Aeneas, and where rich Tullus
  And Ancus fell, we are shadow and dust.
Who knows whether the gods in their high home
  Will add tomorrow's times to today's sum?
But all the gifts, which to your heart you make,
  Your heir with grasping hands can never take.
Once you have perished and your destiny
  Is fixed by Minos and his clear decree,
No eloquence, nobility of birth
  Or piety will bring you back to earth.
From nether gloom Diana cannot free
  Hippolytus, for all his chastity;
By Lethe's stream Pirithous remains,
  For Theseus is too weak to break his chains.

IV.8
To C.Marcius Censorinus
Donarem pateras grataque commodus

I'd willingly give bowls and gifts of bronze
To all my good friends and companions;
I would give tripods, prizes which the brave
Greeks win: the very best of these you'd have,
If only I were rich in works of art
That Scopas and Parrhasius create,–
For one in marble, one with colours could
Produce the likeness of a man or god.
But this is not my strength, and these are toys
Which you don't need by circumstance or choice.
You enjoy odes, and odes I can donate:
A price for my gift I will even state.

No marble statue inscribed with public praise,
By which the spirit and their former days
Return to dead princes, nor the retreat
Of Hannibal in haste, nor any threat
Flung back at him, nor impious Carthage's fire,
Lit by him, who in saving Africa
Received its surname, more clearly declare
One's praise than Muses from Calabria.
And if the writing-paper does not say
What good you've done, you won't have had your pay!
What would become of Troy and Mars's son,
If silence, envious and taciturn,
Prevented the just fame of Romulus?
From river Styx was rescued Aeacus,
Whom virtue, popularity and the tongue
Of mighty poets consecrates among
The blessed isles. The Muse will not let die
The praiseworthy, but lauds them to the sky.
So doughty Hercules is asked as guest
By Jupiter to attend his choicest feast,
The bright stars of Castor and Pollux keep
Men's storm-tossed ships from waters of the deep,
And with green vine-shoots garlanding his brow
Liber brings good results to mortal vow.

IV.9
To Lollius
Ne forte credas interitura, quae

Lest you may think that all my words will die
Which, by arts not divulged to man before,
  I marry to the chords of my guitar,
    Born by the resonant river Aufidus, I:

Though Homer occupies the highest place,
To forget Pindar's music would be wrong,
  Alcaeus' menacing odes and Cean song
    And Stesichorus's important lays.

The years have not destroyed, as they expire,
The songs Anacreon played; the love still breathes,
  And passion's vital heat still lives and seethes
    In Sappho's songs for the Aeolian lyre.

Spartan Helen was not the only wife
Whose heart burned at the finely coiffured hair
  And gilded clothes of an adulterer,
    His courtiers and his regal way of life.

Teucer was not the first with Cretan bow
To fire arrows; not only once did war
  Vex Ilium, and other men before
    Idomeneus and Sthenelus did go

And fight battles fit for the Muses' voice;
Ardent Deiphobus and fierce Hector
  Were not the first to suffer wounds of war
    For their chaste womenfolk and for their boys.

Before King Agamemnon brave men lived,
Many, but all are weighed down by long night;
  They are unwept, and no-one knows their plight,
    For of a holy bard they are deprived.

Concealed virtue is not so far away
From buried idleness. My song-sheets will
  Not leave you unadorned, in silence still;
    I could not suffer with impunity,

Your many labours, Lollius, to enjoy
A blue-black harvest of forgetfulness.
   You have a practised mind, which under stress
      And in fair times straight methods does employ;

You are resolved to punish greed and fraud,
To abstain from wealth, which gathers all in train,
   And not just one year's consulate to gain,
      But, while good and true judgment have ensured

That honesty precedes expedience,
With head held high to fling back corrupt bribes,
   And, victorious, through all the opposing tribes,
      Open the way for your own armaments.

He who possesses much, you would not choose
To call blessed; more properly, he receives
   The name of blessed, who, all that heaven gives,
      Can competently and with wisdom use,

And knows how to endure hard penury,
And fears a shameful act more than life's end;
   He's not afraid to die for a dear friend
      Or perish for the sake of his country.

IV.10
To Ligurinus
O crudelis adhuc et Veneris muneribus potens

Still you are cruel, although the gifts of love
Through Venus' potency you could provide,
But soon the beard of manhood will remove,–
Against your hopes,– all of your boyhood's pride.
Your hair, which now upon your shoulder flows,
Will lose its substance and will fall away;
Your colour, now more lovely than a rose
Blooming with scarlet blossoms, will decay.
Then, when your beard bristles, you'll say, "Alas!"
Mourning the altered aspect you employ,
Whenever you peer in the looking-glass:
"Why had I not today's mind as a boy?
   And why, when I these new attentions seek,
      Does former purity not grace my cheek?"

IV.11
To Phyllis
Est mihi nonum superantis annum

I've a full jar of Alban wine,
  Phyllis, that's over nine years old,
And parsley you can intertwine
  For garlands, and my gardens hold

Ivy to bind your shining hair.
  The silver smiles within my home;
Chaste vervain decks my old altar,
  Which craves the sacrifice of a lamb;

Hither and thither servants hurry;
  The slave boys run and busy girls,
And rolling flames flicker and carry
  Black smoke, which up the chimney curls.

Please understand this joyful date!
  You're called to keep the Ides with me,
Which April's mid-point celebrate,
  The month of Venus of the Sea.

This truly is a solemn day,
  Almost more sacred, it appears,
Than my own birthday: from today
  Maecenas counts his flowing years.

Telephus, whom you like to chase,
  Is not the sort that you can gain;
He's owned by a rich, playful lass,
  Who keeps him on a pleasant chain.

Phaethon's scorching by Jove's flame
  Scares off high hopes; the winged flight
Of Pegasus is a grave paradigm,
  For he threw off his earthly knight,

Bellerophon. Keep to what is fit,
  Do not unequal loves approve,
Don't hope beyond a fair limit!
  Come to me now, my own last love,–

No other love will keep me warm,–
  And learn the music! Come along,
And with your lovely voice perform!
  Dark cares will become less with song.

IV.12
To Virgil

Iam veris comites, quae mare temperant

Now, spring's companions who calm the sea,
The Thracian breezes, into the sails blow,
And now no pastures freeze, nor winter snow
    Swells rivers roaring in cacophony.

The unhappy swallow builds her nest and sings
Weeping for Itys and the eternal shame
Of Cecrops' house, when she abused her name
    Avenging the barbaric lusts of kings.

Now, to the pipe, guardians of fat sheep play
Their songs upon the young and tender sward,
And so they charm the god, who loves the herd
    And the dark hillsides of Arcadia.

The season has brought on a thirst, Virgil:
If vintage pressed at Cales is your plan,
As you are sponsored by young noblemen,
    You'll have to give perfume for your wine-bill!

A little onyx jar of nard will buy
A flask, which now lies in Sulpicius' store,
To give new hopes in generous measure or
    To wash the bitter taste of cares away.

If you are keen for these joys, quickly come
With your own merchandise; it's not my intent
To soak you in my cups without payment,
    Like a rich man who has a well-stocked home.

But put aside delays and thoughts of gain;
Remember, while you may, death's darker fire,
And high thoughts with brief foolishness inspire:
    It's sweet at times to have a fuddled brain!

IV.13
To Lyce

Audivere, Lyce, di mea vota, di

The gods have heard my prayers; you're getting old.
  The gods have heard, and still, Lyce, Lyce,
You wish to be a beauty to behold,–
  You frolic and you drink immoderately

And, in your cups, with tremulous song you seek
  To awake slow Cupid. But he's out on guard,
Upon the girl from Chios' lovely cheek,–
  And she's in bloom and can play the guitar!

Disdainfully, he flies past withered oaks.
  He shrinks from you because, it must be said,
Your stained and yellow teeth ruin your looks,
  Those wrinkles and the snow-white of your head.

No robes of Coan purple now remain,
  No precious gems recall those times you passed,
Which are now filed in the public domain
  Where winged day has imprisoned them at last.

Where are your lover's charms, the way you moved,
  The colour of your skin? Where did they flee?
What's left of her, of her who breathed and loved,
  And with her love stole my own self from me?

I tasted your fruits after Cinara's,–
  You were the epitome of gracious arts;
But fate gave Cinara a few brief years,
  And yet to Lyce a long life imparts,

Just like a small, old crow, – so young men could,
  When hot and glowing, roar excessively
With laughter, as they see a torch of wood
  Dissolve in ashes and then slip away.

IV.14

To Augustus Caesar

Quae cura patrum quaeve Quiritium

How will the Senate and People of Rome
  Perpetuate, Augustus, and record
Through inscriptions and texts for years to come
  Your virtue with fair honour's full reward,–

Wherever the sun lights habitable shores,
  Greatest of all princes, o Emperor?
From you the rough Vindelici learned the laws
  Of Latium and your potency in war.

For, with your soldiers, Drusus more than once
  Threw down the Genaunians' impatient race
And swift Breunians, and, from fearsome mounts,
  Hurled Alpine castles down with eager face.

Soon, the older Nero commenced battle grave
  And drove the monstrous Raetians from the field;
To him the heavens auspicious omens gave,–
  His glory in Mars' contest was revealed.

Oh, to what great destruction he consigned
  Hearts that were sworn to death or liberty,
Almost like Auster, the burning south-wind,
  Who stirs the untamed waves upon the sea,

When the fair chorus of the Pleiades
  Breaks through the clouds; so quick was he, indeed,
To vex the squadrons of his enemies
  And through the fire's heart ride his neighing steed.

So, rolling, bull-shaped Aufidus appears,
  Who past Apulian Daunus' kingdom flows,
When he goes wild and fearful floods prepares
  To devastate the tilled fields and meadows.

Thus, at his vast assault against the foe,
  The iron-clad columns fell to Claudius;
Their first and then their last, down he did mow
  And strewed the ground, a victor without loss.

But you, Augustus, did the troops provide,
  The strategy and your gods. For, on the date
When suppliant Alexandria opened wide
  Her ports and her deserted palace gate,

Propitious Fortune, after fifteen years,
  Gave to your wars a favourable end
And brought the praise and glory Rome desires
  On the accomplishment of your command.

You, the Cantabrian untamed before,
  Mede, Indian and Scythian in flight,
You, all these nations worship and adore,
  Guardian of Italy and Roman might.

You, Nile who hides the sources of his springs,
  You, Hister and Tigris who swiftly runs,
You, Ocean hears, who alive with monstrous things
  Crashes against the far-removed Britons.

You, Gaul's land which no funerals affright,
  You, the earth of hard Iberia obeys;
Sygambrians, who in massacre delight,
  Lay down their arms and sing you hymns of praise.

IV.15
The Augustan age
Phoebus volentem proelia me loqui

When Phoebus saw I wished to tell the tale
  Of battles and of foreign victories,
He beat his lyre and warned me not to sail
  With my small rig across the Tuscan seas.

The Augustan age our rich crops reinstates
  And to our Jove Rome's standards now restores,
Torn down from Parthia's haughty temple gates:
  The age has closed Janus's warless doors.

The licence, which can strict rules override,
  Has been curbed by restrictions and commands;
This age has pushed aside both guilt and crime,
  And ancient arts and skills it now demands.

Through these the Latin name and Italy's strength
  Have grown, her fame and empire's majesty,
Which to the eastern sun stretches its length
  From the sun's couch beneath the western sea.

With Caesar as our institutions' guard,
  No civil rage or force will drive out peace;
No, nor the anger which hammers out the sword
  And brings hostilities to sad cities.

No drinkers of the Danube's waters deep
  Will break your Julian edicts, nor Chinese,
Getans, or Persians who no trust can keep,
  Nor men raised by the river Tanais.

Surrounded by the bounties Liber gives,
  We, both on common and on holy day,
Together with our children and our wives,
  After we first to heaven with due rites pray,

Will sing how, with their fathers' attributes,
  Our princes have the crown of virtue won,
And then, accompanied by Lydian flutes,
  Of Troy, Anchises and kind Venus' son.

Notes

The purpose of these notes is to provide background information, by which the odes can be better understood, rather than literary comment.

I.1

Maecenas became Horace's friend and patron after they had been introduced in to one another in Rome in 38 BC. About two years later he gave Horace a country estate in the Sabine hills near Rome. Born of an apparently distinguished Etruscan family, Caius Cilnius Maecenas was a Roman knight. Maecenas became a senior associate of Octavian, Julius Caesar's adopted son. He acted as one of the confidential mediators at Brundisium (Brindisi) in 40 BC, when the threat of civil war between Octavian and Mark Antony was averted, and Antony agreeed to take the east, while Octavian took the west. Subsequently, Octavian became *princeps* or head-of-state and was known as Augustus, or Augustus Caesar, having received that title in 27 BC. For further background, see Introduction.

The sea of Myrtos was the southern Aegean Sea. Massic wine came from southern Campania in Italy. The Marsians were a Latin people, who lived around Lake Fucinus.

Euterpe and Polyhymnia were two of the Greek Muses, goddesses of music, poetry and song. Lesbos was the home of the Greek lyric poets of the late seventh century BC, the male Alcaeus and the female Sappho. A description of the seven-stringed lyre is given in the note to I.32.

I.2

Horace was born in 65 BC and the Roman republic had been torn by civil conflict for most of his life. Horace, who published the first three books of odes in 23 BC, dutifully chose Augustus as the subject of this ode immediately following the prologue to his patron and sponsor Maecenas. In it he hails the head of state as a sort of messiah after a period of turmoil and ill omen.

Pyrrha was the wife of Deucalion, known for the flood which Jupiter sent in his days. Proteus was a sea-god who served Neptune. Tiber was, and is, the river of Rome, and the Etruscan, or Tuscan, shore is its northern bank.

The state religion in Rome involved the worship of the traditional Olympian gods of Greece under their Latin names. Jupiter is equivalent to Zeus; Apollo to Phoebus Apollo; Venus to Aphrodite; Mercury to Hermes, whose mother was Maia, Jupiter being the father. Mars was the Roman god of war; Vesta was another name for Cybele, the earth mother (see I.16).

Venus was sometimes known as the goddess of Eryx in Sicily where there was a famous temple dedicated to her. Ilia was a poetic name for Rhea Silvia, the mother, by Mars, of Romulus, the legendary founder of Rome.

I.3

This and the following four odes, to I.7 inclusive, continue Horace's plan of addressing distinguished individuals in Augustan Rome. Virgil was the great epic poet of the Augustan age. Having made his reputation with his Eclogues, a series of poems on pastoral themes, he then wrote the Georgics, a set of four books in Latin hexameter verse on the subject of farming. He began his great epic work the Aeneid in 30 BC. This was the story of Aeneas, a Trojan hero, who escaped from the burning city of Troy and, after many adventures, landed in Italy, where he defeated the indigenous Etruscans. The Aeneid was still not entirely finished on Virgil's death in 19 BC.

A friend of Horace, Virgil had introduced him to Maecenas. Virgil made more than one voyage to Athens, possibly to research his great epic poem.

Castor and Pollux were more than just heroes who became stars. The sons of Leda by Jupiter, they were considered to be divine protectors of seafarers (see IV.8). A temple was decided to them in Rome in 484 BC, being later rebuilt between 7 BC and 6 AD. Aeolus was said to keep the winds imprisoned in caverns, releasing them at Jupiter's request. For Iapyx, the west/north-westerly wind which blew from Italy towards Greece, see also III.27.

The Hyades were a group of seven stars in the head of the constellation Taurus. Epirus, now part of Albania, had a rocky promontory called Acroceraunia, or Thunder-Heights, which ran out into the Ionian Sea.

Prometheus formed men clay and animated them with fire stolen from heaven. For his punishment, see II.13. Daedalus was the father of Icarus, who flying with his father, went too close to the sun: the wax on his wings melted and he perished in the sea. Acheron was a name for the underworld, to which the dead were transported.

I.4

This ode is known as Horace's first spring ode, the second being IV.7. It was addressed to Sestius, one of the two consuls in office in Rome at the time of the publication of the first three books of odes in 23 BC. Sestius did not start the year as consul, but was appointed as a substitute for Augustus when the latter suffered a serious illness after the Murena affair (see Introduction and II.10). In his early political career Sestius had been a supporter of Brutus, the assassin of Julius Caesar, Octavian's adoptive father, when serving as *quaestor*, a rank of magistrates responsible for treasury affairs.

The consulate was the highest formal office in the Roman republic. Two consuls served together for one year, the minimum qualification traditionally having been that they should have moved through various junior magistracies and reached their forty-third year. After the consulship they would attain proconsular rank and often serve as governors of Rome's overseas provinces. After the civil wars these rules were varied, as the death of many citizens of good family during the civil wars left a depleted generation which could present fewer candidates. Augustus, after his victory over Mark Antony (see Introduction), held the consulate without a break from 31 BC until his illness in 23 BC.

Venus, the goddess of love was called Cytherean after the island of Cythera in the Aegean Sea, celebrated for her worship. There were three Graces. Vulcan, the fire-god, was the son of Jupiter and Juno. The one-eyed Cyclopes were giants who worked in his smithy. For Faunus, see I.17 and the hymn at III.18. Pluto was the king of the underworld.

I.5

The Pyrrha ode is the first love ode in Horace's collection of poems and consists of sixteen concise lines in the original Latin.

Today, in the Arsenale museum in Venice, one can still see crudely-painted, small, rectangular plaques, dating from the middle ages, which were offered in church by sailors after a safe return.

I.6

Marcus Agrippa had commanded Octavian's troops on land and sea in the 30s, winning many significant victories. In the constitutional settlement of 27 BC Octavian became head-of-state with the title Augustus and gave Agrippa responsibility for constructing a number of important new buildings in Rome, including the original Pantheon, the Baths of Agrippa and the Saepta Julia, or voting enclosure. Agrippa married Augustus' daughter Julia.

The poet Varius' works do not survive. Varius had been with Virgil in 38 BC when Horace was introduced to Maecenas.

Odysseus, Achilles, Meriones and Diomedes were heroes of the Trojan War. Pelops was the father of Atreus and Thyestes and grandfather of

Agamemnon and Menelaus. His name was given to the Peloponnese. Thyestes served up to Atreus the flesh of his son.

I.7

Horace may have visited some, or even all, the Greek sites referred to here, when he was a young student in Athens or serving with Brutus before the battle of Actium. Virgin Pallas' town was Athens, whose goddess was Pallas Athene. Her statue was in the Parthenon on the Acropolis, which overlooked the city. The fountain of Albunea, the river Anio and the town of Tibur were near Horace's Sabine farm.

The ode becomes a vehicle for a set piece by Teucer, the banished son of Telamon, king of Salamis.

Munatius Plancus, the ode's addressee, was a veteran statesman who had served under both Julius Caesar and Mark Antony. He become consular governor of Asia and, later, Syria and joined Octavian's forces in 32 BC because of his hostility towards Cleopatra, the subject of I.37. Plancus is known through his correspondence with the Roman statesman and author Cirero to have been a sophisticated individual, and it was he who proposed the name of Augustus for Octavian at the time of the constitutional settlement in 27 BC. However, Plancus also had a reputation as a turncoat and it was suggested that he had been implicated in the proscription and political murder of his brother some thirteen years earlier. Perhaps Horace implies that he, like Teucer, was innocent of the accusation against him.

I.8

The son of the goddess Thetis was Achilles, the great warrier of Greece in the Trojan War and the subject of the Iliad, the epic poem by Homer. There was a legend that Achilles once dressed in a young girl's clothes at Scyros, in order to escape detection. Lycia was a country in Asia Minor, today's Turkey, and supported Troy in the Trojan War. For yellow Tiber, see II.3.

I.9

Thaliarchus was Greek for "Master of Festivities" and the name could refer either to a wine steward or Major Domo, or be used of a friend (see note II.7). Soracte was a mountain in Etruria, north of Rome.

The word "plus" may give a clue to the Horatian wit which subtly pervades the last three stanzas. Although scholars appear not to have recognised this possibility and a more neutral interpretation is acceptable, it should be noted that the terms "claimed", "appointed hour" and "pledge" could all be used in banking in the context of the recovery of loans due. In this case, the nuance appears to be that the addressee should claim the dues which youth owes him. Horace's father had been a debt-collector and banker and Horace began his career as a treasury official. See also "tag" and "subtracts" in II.5, "credit" in I.3 and I.24, and "shortages" in III.24.

I.10

Mercury, the Greek Hermes, was the winged messenger of the gods. Scholars have noted that this poem is strongly influenced by the poet Alcaeus of Lesbos. In II.7 Horace gives Mercury credit for having saved him at the battle of Philippi. The god is also connected with banking, the profession of Horace's father.

I.11

The name Leuconoe seems to be contrived from the Greek as a sort of character-pun. Literally it means "white-minded", perhaps signifying "empty-headed". Other examples of names contrived to establish mood or character are Thaliarchus in I.5, Neobule in III.12 and Lyce in IV.13.

The charts of Babylon were similar to astrology today.

In the last line, the Latin reads "*carpe diem*", one of Horace's most famous and memorable phrases.

I.12

This ode in honour of Augustus has similarities in content and Latin metre with I.2. It looks back to a golden age of courage and probity in Rome. By contrast with today's religious beliefs in the Judaeo-Christian tradition, where a better era is expected in the future rather than looked back to in the past, classical Greece and Rome looked to an earlier age to find examples of a better society. The ode places Augustus on a pinnacle, second only to Jupiter, provided the "*princeps*" can defeat Rome's eastern foes.

Clio was the Muse of history. Mount Helicon in Boeotia was sacred to Apollo and the Muses. Pindus, regarded as the home of the Muses, was in Thessaly. Haemus was a mountain range in Thrace where the mythical singer Orpheus lived. Leda's sons were Castor and Pollux (see I.3).

Romulus was the mythical founder of Rome. Pompilius was Rome's second king and Tarquin its fifth. Cato was famed for his fortitude (see II.1). For Regulus, see III.5. The Scauri were a distinguished Roman family. Paulus the consul fell at the battle of Cannae in 216 BC. Fabricius led the Romans against Pyrrhus in 280 BC. A Lar was a household god.

Marcellus was a hero of the Second Punic War. Marcellus was also the name of August's nephew (see Introduction and note to II.10) and likely heir until his untimely death. Like other members of the imperial family he was from the Julian *gens* or tribe.

I.13

Lydia was the addressee of I.8, where she had turned the head of Sybaris. It is not necessary to believe that she was a real person, although she could have been.

In Rome at that period, the liver was believed to be the seat of the emotions, and the verb "to burn" was used to describe romantic passion. Nectar was the drink of the gods, their food being ambrosia.

I.14

In this allegorical poem intended to support Augustus' regime, Horace expresses fears that Rome will again face political disruption and instability. The supreme power, which Augustus held, did not leave him without enemies among some aristocratic families.

The Cyclades were a group of islands around Delos in the Aegean Sea off eastern Greece.

I.15

Like the Teucer speech in I.7, the speech by Nereus the prophet seems to be influenced by Horace's education in Rome and Athens, where rhetoric and advocacy were taught as disciplines. Juno's speech in III.3 is another example of a dramatic set-piece.

The shepherd is Paris, the son of King Priam of Troy, who had stolen Helen from her husband, Menelaus of Sparta, so precipitating the Trojan War. Ida was a mountain near Troy where Paris tended sheep and where he carried out the famous judgment of Paris, adjudicating between the beauty of the Greek goddesses Hera, Athene and Aphrodite. Paris awarded the prize, a golden apple, to Aphrodite, for she told him of Helen's beauty, and so he incurred the wrath of the other two goddesses, who determined that Troy should be destroyed. Wood from Ida was used to build Paris's ships. Nereus was a sea-god. Among the various Greek heroes, the son of Laertes is Ulysses or, in his Greek form, Odysseus. The son of Tydeus was Diomedes. He, like Meriones, is referred to in I.6. For Nestor, see II.9.

I.16

Dindymene was the goddess Vesta or Cybele, sometimes known in Rome as Magna Mater or Great Mother. She was identified with the earth and the earth's fertility. Apollo is called Pythian because Pytho was the original name for Delphi, which received that name after Apollo killed a python or serpent there. Delphi, located high above the northern shore of the Gulf of Corinth, became the sacred home of the Oracle and the Pythian Games. Liber is an ancient Italian deity, later identified with the Greek Bacchus or Dionysus, god of wine and the irrational. The Corybantes were priests of Cybele, whose religious worship included wild and noisy music and dance. For Prometheus, see I.3. For Thyestes, son of Pelops, see note I.6.

I.17

Horace brings us to his Sabine farm, the estate which Maecenas gave him. In some of his other poetic works, the Epistles and the Satires, Horace records that eight slaves were employed on his farm and that there were five tenant-farms on the estate as a whole.

Faunus was, by Latin tradition, the protecting deity of agriculture and shepherds. Later he was identified with the Greek god Pan and represented with horns and goats' feet. See I.4 and III.18.

We know nothing of Tyndaris. Teos was the birthplace of the Greek lyric poet Anacreon. Penelope was the wife of Ulysses, whose Greek name was Odysseus, the hero of Homer's Odyssey. Circe was a beautiful sea-nymph with magical powers who fell in love with Ulysees on his travels but failed to hold him. Lesbos was the birthplace of Sappho and Alcaeus, the Greek lyric poets.

I.18

Varus is possibly the Quintilius Varus who is mourned in I.24. Tibur is today's Tivoli, to the east of Rome in a valley below the Sabine hills. Horace would have had to go through it on the way up to his farm and is believed eventually to have had a house there. Catilus was the legendary founder of Tibur. The Centaurs were half-horse, half-man. They fought the Lapiths, a Thessalian mountain people, at the wedding of Hippodamia to Pirithous their king. The battle was commemorated on the frieze of the Parthenon, the great temple on the Acropolis of Athens, which Horace will have known from his student days.

Bacchus, the god of wine, also had the names Euhius and Bassareus. The Sithonians came from a town in Thrace, the birthplace of one of Horace's girl friends, Chloe of III.26. Berecyntus was a mountain in Asia Minor sacred to Cybele (see III.19 and IV.1).

I.19

Glycera also appears in I.30, again in company with Venus, the goddess of love. Her name is derived from the Greek adjective for "sweet". She appears again in I.33 and III.19. Bacchus, the god of wine and the irrational, was the son of Semele, a daughter of Cadmus the mythical king of Thebes. Bacchus' father was Jupiter. For the Parthians and their "Parthian shot", see II.13.

In the last lines of the ode Horace describes the materials needed for a simple sacrifice to the goddess. The fresh turf, which he asks his servants to bring, would have been for a makeshift altar.

I.20

Horace offers his patron Maecenas some modest hospitality, the local Sabine wine being contrasted with the Falernian vintages from Campania or wine from the hills of Formiae near the coast of Latium.

Horace put down his wine some years previously, when Maecenas had just recovered from an illness. This illness and Maecenas' tumultuous reception in the theatre is also mentioned in II.17.

I.21

Horace called his odes "*carmina*" or songs, and some contain references to musical accompaniment. Many, however, may have been intended to be read rather than sung. This hymn, addressed to Diana and Apollo, was almost certainly composed to be sung to music by the girls and boys.

Diana was originally a Latin goddess, but was later identified with the Greek Artemis, the goddess of hunting. Cynthius was another name for Apollo. Lato or Latona was their mother and Jove or Jupiter their father.

Algidus was a wooded mountain south-east of Rome. Erymanthus was a range of mountains in Arcadia in Greece. Cragos was a mountain chain in Lycia. For Tempe, see I.7. Delos was an island in the Aegean sacred to Apollo.

I.22

Aristius Fuscus appears in both the Epistles and the Satires as an amusing friend of Horace. This seems to confirm the humorous intent behind the ode.

The Syrtes were sand-banks off the north coast of Africa. The Caucasus mountains are between the Black Sea and the Caspian Sea. Hydaspes was a tributary of the river Indus. Daunia was a Roman province in central Italy, named after King Daunus (see III.30). Numidia was in the area of the modern Algeria. Lalage reappears in II.5.

I.23

The young deer of this ode can be compared with the heifer of II.5. Gaetulia was where Morocco is today. For Chloe, see III.9. and III.26. She was from Sithone in Thrace.

I.24

Virgil was Horace's friend, the great poet of the Augustan age who wrote the Eclogues, the Georgics and the Aeneid. Quintilius was perhaps the Varus of I.18, but this is not certain. There were many members of this family during the Augustan period and further details are given in chapter 23 of Sir Ronald Syme's "The Augustan Aristocracy" (see Bibliography).

Virgil is also the addressee of IV.12.

Melpomene is the Muse of tragic poetry and song, and is also addressed at the end of III.30. Orpheus was the mythical minstrel from Thrace and the husband of Eurydice (see I.2).

I.25

A younger Lydia appears in I.13. They are not necessarily the same person, or even real persons. Similar characters are Barine in II.8, Chloris in III.15 and Lyce in IV.3.

Ivy and myrtle were both evergreen, being related to Bacchus and Venus respectively. They were used in crowns or garlands for celebration. The river Hebrus was in Thrace in northern Greece.

I.26

Horace expresses his indifference to foreign affairs. The king of the northern shore could by Cotiso of III.8 and the shore could be the north-west coast of the Black Sea. Tiridates was a prince of Parthia, to the east and north of today's Syria. He was supported by Augustus and twice took refuge in Rome. He was hostile to Phraates IV, who is referred to in II.2.

Lamia is probably the Aelius Lamia of III.17, who was appointed as Augustus' senior praetorian legate in Spain in 24 BC. There he was responsible for the region of Tarragona and three or four legions. I.36 and II.12 are also addressed to individuals named Lamia who, in spite of some scholarly dispute, may be the same person.

The Muse is called Pimplean after a location near the Pierian spring not far from Mount Olympus on the border of Macedonia and Thessaly. Lesbos was the birthplace of Sappho and Alcaeus (see also I.17).

I.27

The scene is a drinking party which is about to get out of control. For Falernian wine, see I.20, Opus was in town in Locris in Greece.

Pegasus was the winged horse which carried Bellerophon when he killed the Chimaera, a fire-vomiting monster, part lion, part dragon and part goat.

I.28

Archytas lived in Tarentum, a Spartan settlement in southern Italy. He was a mathematician of the fourth century BC, who studied the nature and size of the universe. He had been a pupil of Pythagoras, the son of Panthous. Pythagoras is said to have believed that, in an earlier incarnation, he had been the warrior Euphorbus, who fought in the Trojan War. For Pelops, whose father was Tantalus, see I.6. For Tantalus, see II.13. Tithonus was turned into a cicada. Minos became a judge in the underworld.

Proserpina's duty in the underworld was to cut off a lock of hair from the dead. For the constellation Orion, which set in November, an often stormy season, see also II.13 and III.27. Venusia was the birthplace of Horace. The Matine shore, beneath Mount Matinus, was also in Apulia.

Sophocles' tragedy *Antigone* underlines the religious importance attached by Greeks of the classical period to receiving a burial, however symbolic.

I.29

Iccius was probably planning to join the Arabian campaign of Aelius Gallus in 26 BC. Iccius reappears in Horace's Epistle I.12 as Agrippa's steward in Sicily, where he was responsible for collecting rents from Agrippa's estates. Sheba was in the region of today's Yemen.

Panaetius was a Stoic philosopher of the first century BC. The Academy refers to the Socratic school, which perpetuated the teachings of Socrates, the Athenian philosopher of the late fifth century BC whose philosophy and dialectic were immortalised through the writings of his pupil Plato.

I.30

Venus is identified with the Greek goddess Aphrodite, who had centres of worship at Cnidos in Asia Minor (see note III.28) and Paphos in Cyprus. Glycera appeared previously in I.19 and appears again in I.33 and III.19. Hermes was the Greek name for the Roman god Mercury.

I.31

Horace wrote this ode on the occasion of the consecration of the new Temple of Apollo on the Palatine Hill in Rome on 9 October 28 BC. Apollo was believed to have assisted Octavian's naval forces in their victory at Actium off the west coast of Greece on 2 September 31 BC. In this engagement Antony and Cleopatra, characterised by their opponents as representing the forces of the east, were defeated. I.37 describes Cleopatra's subsequent death.

The new temple, of which a few ruins still stand, was an important element in the magnificent rebuilding programme in Rome initiated by Octavian before he received the title Augustus.

Horace, as a student in his early twenties, had originally supported Brutus, the murderer of Julius Caesar, the adoptive father of Octavian, but was pardoned in the subsequent amnesty (see Introduction).

I.32

Horace acknowledges his debt to Alcaeus, the Greek lyric poet from Lesbos who lived around 610 BC. Alcaeus lived during a period of civil wars on Lesbos and supported the radical movement against the established tyrants. See also II.13. Liber is here equivalent to Bacchus whose Greek name was Dionysus.

The Greek lyre, which came to have seven strings, was made from an inverted and scooped-out tortoiseshell. From this a pair of horns was extended, and between the horns a transverse piece of wood was fixed. The strings were stretched from the bottom edge of the tortoiseshell to the transverse piece of wood, and were then tuned.

I.33

Tibullus was an elegiac poet in Rome and many of his poems still survive. The names of Horace's ladies may or may not be fictitious, but they are Greek rather than Roman. This is probably a reflection on prevailing Roman views of morality, Roman girls being considered suitable for marriage and motherhood, Greek girls for play. Another aspect of Horace's position was that he was the son of a freedman. Although his talents as a poet won him the patronage of Maecenas and the support of Augustus, he was not in a position to marry above his class, but probably not keen to marry within it. The pleasure of female company was provided through other means, often by Greek or Thracian immigrant musicians or courtesans. For Glycera, see I.19. Pholoe reappears in II.5.

I.34

The "senseless wisdom" once practised by Horace was Epicureanism, which taught not only the importance of human pleasure, but that natural phenomena had entirely rational explanations. This is the reason for Horace writing of thunder and lightning in a cloudless sky. The point is that Jupiter had the power to overturn what might have been considered the rational laws of science.

For Styx, see II.14. The phrase "Atlas' bounds" probably refers to the limits of the known world. In myth, the god Atlas supported the heavens from the mountains of north-west Africa.

I.35

Antium, the site of a temple dedicated to the goddess Fortune, was about 50 miles south of Rome. There was a Temple of Fortune & Dawn in Rome from an early period. A temple of Fortune dating from 130-100 BC still survives in Praeneste (today's Palestrina) not far from Horace's Sabine farm.

If Augustus ever had it in mind to invade Britain, the invasion did not take place. There were other priorities in Gaul and Spain. The expedition to the Red Sea is probably that led by Aelius Gallius in 26

BC, which Iccius of I.29 planned to join. The Dacians lived in the area of today's Rumania and Hungary. The Scythians were a nomadic people who roamed the steppes of Ukraine and beyond. The Massagetae were a Scythian people who lived to the east of the Caspian Sea, in the region of today's Mongolia.

I.36

Nothing is known of Numida, who had been on military service in Spain, probably confronting the Cantabrians referred to in II.11. His friend Lamia may have been the Lamia of I.26 who served as a legate in Spain, or, conceivably, a younger relative. See I.26 and III.17.

The toga was the outer garment worn by adult Roman males during peace-time. It consisted of a single long and broad piece of cloth, which was wrapped around the shoulders and body in a flowing style. To mark something in Cretan chalk, known for its whiteness, was a reference rather similar to today's red-letter day. The Salians, or "Leapers", were a religious college of priests dedicated to the service of Mars; they were known for their lively dancing.

In the party, which was planned, Damalis and Bassus were to compete in an "*amystis*", a drinking contest in which all the wine in a goblet was drained at a single gulp.

I.37

Cleopatra was the Queen of Egypt and the consort of Mark Antony. After the murder of Julius Caesar in 44 BC Antony and Octavian had been allies, defeating the troops of Brutus and Cassius at Philippi two years later. Subsequently, at the peace of Brundisium in 40 BC, they divided most of the empire between them, Antony taking the east, where he came under Cleopatra's influence. Eventually, Octavian and Antony, and east and west could no longer live in harmony. Antony gave Rome's eastern territories to Cleopatra and her sons in 34 BC and hostilities followed. In 32 BC Octavian drove Antony's supporters out of Rome and declared war on Cleopatra. A sea battle took place at Actium, off the west coast of Greece, on 2 September 31 BC. Antony and Cleopatra were defeated and fled. They returned to Alexandria, where the following year Antony committed suicide, to be followed a few days later, on 10 August 30 BC, by Cleopatra, as Roman troops approached. These events were pivotal in giving Octavian mastery of the ancient world. Horace's account, though not entirely accurate historically, expresses the excitement and drama of Cleopatra's defeat and death. See also Introduction.

I.38

The disparaging reference to Persian decoration is perhaps a deliberate sequel to the Cleopatra ode, I.37. The defeated Mark Antony had not been well regarded for having adopted eastern costume and manners. The addressee is a slave-boy.

In Book II, repeating the pattern of Book I, Horace uses the first three odes to address distinguished personages.

Pollio, who was born in 76 BC, had seen military service under Julius Caesar and was later a senior officer in Gaul, where he was in charge of some legions loyal to Mark Antony. Before the accommodation at Brundisium in 40 BC between Mark Antony and Octavian, Pollio declined a request from Mark Antony's brother Lucius Antonius to attack Octavian's troops. Shortly thereafter, Octavian and Antony agreed, with Maecenas acting as mediator, that they should split the military control of the empire, Antony taking the east. Within a few months, Pollio became consul in Rome at the age of only 36, probably as a reward for his prudence. After his consulate he led an army to victory over the Dalmatians in Illyria, a critical land route from Italy to the east. He was awarded a triumph in 39 BC. He then withdrew from public life and devoted himself to literature. He was the addressee of Virgil's fourth Eclogue, is said to have been founded a public library in Rome and wrote a "History of the Civil Wars" which does not survive.

Metellus was consul in 60 BC, the year when Julius Caesar, Pompey and Crassus formed an alliance now known as the First Triumvirate, which had much the same purpose as the Second Triumvirate between Octavian, Mark Antony and Lepidus, namely to try to prevent civil war by allocating geographical and military control of the empire to the rival leaders. Neither triumvirate did more than defer the ultimate reckoning.

Cecrops was an ancient king who was said to have founded the acropolis, or citadel, of Athens. Since tragic drama originated in Athens, the high shoe, or buskin, worn by tragic actors is referred to as belonging to Cecrops.

Cato was a supporter of Pompey and committed suicide after Julius Caesar's defeat of the Pompeians at Thapsus in Africa in 46 BC. He later became a symbol of stubborn and high-minded stoicism.

Jugurtha usurped the throne of Numidia in North Africa in 118 BC. His erratic behaviour against Rome over a ten-year period eventually led to war, and his defeat and capture. He was brought as a prisoner to Rome in 105 BC where he met his death.

The Parthians were Rome's enemies in the east. Cea was the birthplace of the greek lyric poet Simonides, who was famed for his poems in honour of the dead.

For the last stanza, compare III.3.

II.2

Sallustius Crispus was the adopted son of the historian Sallust and a grandson of Sallust's sister. The use of both his names may be intended to reinforce Horace's admonishment. Crispus was perhaps already close to the centre of influence at Rome and he later succeeded Maecenas as Augustus' chief adviser on domestic and political affairs, after Maecenas' fall from grace (see Introduction).

Proculeius was the half-brother of Maecenas' wife Terentia. He was also the half-brother of Licinius Murena, a hot-tempered individual who met an untimely death after being implicated in the conspiracy against Augustus in 23 BC. Many scholars believe that Licinius Murena is the Licinius of II.10. Further details of the Murena affair are given there and in the Introduction.

Proculeius' care towards his brothers was not in reference to Licinius, a half-brother, but to two full brothers who had lost their fortune in the civil wars. Proculeius had made generous provision for them.

The Carthaginians originated in Phoenicia in the eastern Mediterranean and had settled in Spain as well as North Africa.

Phraates IV ruled Parthia in the 30s but later lost his throne, recovering it in 26 BC. He was for a time involved in a war against Tiridates, the prince referred to in I.26.

II.3

Quintus Dellius was once described as a "*desultor*" of the civil wars, a "*desultor*" being a circus-performer who vaulted from one horse to another while they were in motion. He served under Mark Antony in Parthia, but, when civil war came, withdrew his allegiance to Mark Antony and joined Octavian before the battle of Actium. He spent his later life writing history, including an account of Antony's Parthian campaign.

Tiber is called yellow because of the colour of the soil in the channel and the adjacent banks. Inachus was the first king of Argos in Greece.

The ferry was the boat on which Charon took the dead across the River Styx to the underworld.

II.4

Phocis was an area of mainland Greece beteen Boeotia and Aetolia. Briseis the slave girl was taken from Achilles by Agamemnon, king of the Greek forces at Troy, as a result of which Achilles sulked in his tent and would not be drawn into the fighting until after the death of his friend Patroclus. Tecmessa was the daughter of king Teuthras and became Ajax' mistress. Atrides, or the son of Atreus, refers to Agamemnon, whose love of Cassandra precipitated his murder by his wife Clytemnestra after his return to Mycenae from Troy. The Thessalians, from the European side of the Bosphorus, are contrasted with the Trojans from the Asian side.

Horace reached the age of forty in 25 BC.

II.5

The name Lalage appears in I.22, Pholoe in I.33 and III.15. The way Roman costume was worn, Chloris' right shoulder would have been exposed rather than both shoulders. Girls were often married in Rome shortly after puberty, so Lalage here may be in her early teens. The implication is that Chloris and Pholoe are women of easy virtue, and this is more than confirmed in III.15, where both reappear.

The financial jargon in stanza 4 can be compared with I.9.

II.6

A letter addressed from Augustus to Horace is quoted by the historian Suetonius: "What sort of recollection I have of you, you will be able to hear from our friend Septimius." This is probably the same Septimius.

Tibur, the current Tivoli, east of Rome, was founded by Tiburtus of Argos. The river Galaesus was near Tarentum on the south coast of Italy. The fleeces of the sheep were considered so valuable that the sheep were protected with leather skins. Phalanthus founded Tarentum in about 700 BC. Hymettus was a mountain near Athens famous for its honey-bees. Venafrum was in Campania. Mount Aulon was near Tarentum. For Falernian wine, see I.20 and elsewhere.

II.7

Pompeius Varus was not Pompey the Great, the foe of Julius Caesar.

After Julius Caesar's assassination, Brutus went to Athens where he attracted a following of young Roman students including Horace, who enlisted as a junior officer. Brutus and his co-conspirator Cassius were defeated at Philippi by Octavian and Mark Antony in 42 BC. After the defeat Horace returned to Rome under amnesty, but Pompeius clearly did not.

Some scholars have suggested that Horace overstates his own cowardice on the battlefield. Certainly the loss of his shield contains echoes of earlier Greek poets and may or may nor be an embellishment. However, as Horace appears to confirm in III.4, the defeat seems to have been a powerful and traumatic experience in his life.

For comments on Mercury, see I.10. Massic wine was produced on what is now Monte Massico in Campania and was highly regarded. The commands which follow are given to servants. For use in garlands, celery is referred to in I.36, myrtle in I.4. There is a drinking party in I.27. The custom was that the guest who threw the highest number on the dice would be master of ceremonies. The Edonians were from Thrace where the heavy drinking of the inhabitants is referred to in I.27.

II.8

No evidence survives to indicate whether Barine was a real person, a pseudonym or imaginary.

II.9

Valgius was a friend of Horace, a scholar and a minor poet. He wrote an uncompleted work on medicinal plants and some elegies of which only fragments survive.

Nestor, king of Pylos, was known for his wisdom and prophecies when he accompanied the Greeks in the Trojan War. Antilochus was his son and was killed by Memnon. Troilus (the subject of Shakespeare's *Troilus and Cressida*) was the son of King Priam of Troy and his wife Hecuba. He was killed by Achilles.

Niphates was apparently in Armenia and the name seems to have referred to both a mountain and its river. Armenia was ceded to Octavian after the victory at Actium and subsequently became a vassal state. The Parthian river was the Euphrates. The Gelonians were a Scythian tribe, who lived in the modern Ukraine, and are referred to again in II.20 and III.4.

II.10

It is possible, but not certain, that the Licinius of this ode is the Licinius Murena who defended Marcus Primus, the proconsul of Macedonia, against a charge of attacking Thrace without authority. Murena, the consul of 23 BC, clashed with Augustus, who had appeared in court in person to counter Primus' claim that his actions had been authorised by Augustus and Augustus' nephew Marcellus. Murena was a man of high temper and, following this clash, seems to have joined a conspiracy organised by Fannius Caepio. He was detected and killed. The arguments for and against this identification are explored by Syme and Quinn (see Bibliography). See also Introduction.

II.11

Quinctius Hirpinus came from a well-known provincial family in Samnium, who had fallen into some obscurity. Asinius Pollio of II.1 married a member of the Quinctius family.

The Cantabrians lived in north-west Spain. Augustus fought a campaign against them in 26 BC. They were not subdued until 19 BC, by Agrippa. The term Scythians was often used as a general designation of nomadic peoples who lived north of the Black Sea.

A red-faced moon was regarded as the sign of stormy weather to come. Assyrian balm is known to have been produced from nard grown in the vale of Jericho and was used for hair-dressing and body-lotion.

II.12

Maecenas, Horace's patron, seems to have proposed that Horace should write epic poetry to celebrate mythical and historical events. Numantia was in north-west Spain and resisted Roman troops from 195 BC until its capture in 133 BC. Hannibal was Rome's enemy in the Second Punic War of 208-201 BC, invading Italy with his elephants before withdrawing to Carthage. Punic, derived from Phoenician, is synonymous with Carthaginian. The blood in the sea of Sicily refers to Roman naval victories in the First Punic War of 264-241 BC. These events are listed by Horace in reverse sequence.

For the Lapiths, see I.18. Hylaeus was a Centaur who attempted to rape Atalanta, but was shot by her. The children of Earth, fathers of the sky, were the Titans, sometimes identified with the Giants who rebelled against Jove. Hercules was called in to subdue them because no Giant could be killed by a god. Saturn, or Cronos, the father of Jove, had supported the Titans.

The third stanza presents an image from a Roman triumph. Licymnia is believed by many scholars to be a pseudonym for Maecenas' wife Terentia. This would add point to the reference. Diana was equivalent to the Greek Artemis, the virgin goddess of hunting. Her holiday was on the Ides of August, the thirteenth of the month.

Achaemenes was the ancestor of the kings of ancient Persia, and the grandfather of Cyrus the Great. Mygdon was a legendary prince of Phrygia in Asia Minor.

II.13

One day, when Horace was walking in his estate, a tree, or perhaps a large branch, fell so close to him that he was in danger of being killed. The event was a serious shock and is mentioned again in II.17, III.4 and III.8.

Colchis was the town of Medea, the sorceress and wife of Jason the Argonaut. The Parthian cavalry were famed for their "Parthian shot": while apparently in retreat, they would suddenly turn their horses and fire volleys of arrows at their pursuing enemy in order to catch them unprotected. See also I.19.

Proserpine was the queen of the underworld and the wife of Pluto (see note I.28). Aeacus, also referred to in III.19, together with Minos and Rhadamanthus, judged the shades of the dead. Sappho and Alcaeus were Greek lyric poets. Aeolia was part of coastal Asia Minor, off which Sappho was born on the island of Lesbos. Alcaeus' songs in time of war are also referred to in I.32.

The hundred-headed hound was Cerberus, who guarded the entrance to the underworld but was subdued by the playing of Orpheus. The Eumenides was a euphemistic name for the Furies. Prometheus created mankind from clay and fire, for which he was chained to a rock and his liver eaten by a bird (see I.3). The father of Pelops was Tantalus, who revealed the secrets of the gods after he had been invited to dine with them (see I.28). His punishment was to be tantalised by being unable to reach the fruit above his head or water beneath his chin, and to suffer eternal hunger and thirst. Orion was a great hunter, who tried to assault Diana, and, having been shot by her, was transported to heaven as a constellation.

II.14

Postumus could have been the senator Propertius Postumus, who at one time left his wife, Aelia Galla, to go to the eastern wars (see Bibliography: Syme).

Pluto was the god of the underworld. Geryon was a mythical giant with three bodies, who lived in the far west. Tityos, also a giant, was a son of Jove. He attempted to seduce the goddess Latona and was punished by being stretched out in the underworld, where a vulture fed on his liver (see also III.4). Styx was the river of the underworld, across which the dead were ferried by Charon. Danaus was the father of fifty daughters, who, with the exception of Hypermnestra, stabbed their husbands to death on their wedding night, For their punishment, see note III.11. Sisyphus, an unprincipled prince of Corinth was killed by Theseus; his punishment in the underworld was to push a rock up-hill, only for it always to roll back down again.

To give point to the last stanza, the Latin for undiluted wine has been translated as port. This is a deliberate anachronism.

II.15

This ode comments on the invasion of the countryside by wealthy Romans building mansions with pools and ornamental gardens. The Lucrine Lake was near Baiae, a seaside community whose overdevelopment is also referred to in II.18.

The plane-tree, an eastern import, was called celibate because, unlike the elm, it was not "married" to vines to give them support. See also IV.5.

Romulus was the mythical founder of Rome, and Cato the Elder was an early statesman and moralist. A ten-foot stick was normally used as a measuring pole by Roman military surveyors.

II.16

Grosphus was Pompeius Grosphus, who, in Horace's Epistle I.12, was introduced to Iccius, the steward of Agrippa's property in Sicily (for Agrippa, the close associate of Augustus, see I.6). Iccius was presumably the same friend who is addressed in I.29. The reference to Sicilian cows in the penultimate stanza suggests that Grosphus himself also lived in Sicily. Horace is likely to have visited the island; in III.4 (see note) he refers to being caught in a storm off Palinurus.

The reference to Care has similarities to the reference to Anxiety in III.1. In both instances the Latin word is "*Cura*". Eurus was the south-east wind.

Tithonus, the consort of Aurora, goddess of the dawn, was granted immortality and, after reaching a decrepit old age, was changed into a cicada (see I.28).

The purple dye was made from the juice of the murex, or African purple-fish.

II.17

This ode shows the depth of the affection in which Horace held Maecenas, going beyond the expected loyalty of a client towards a generous patron. Horace's prophecy in the third stanza was virtually fulfilled. He died a few weeks after Maecenas in 8 BC (see Introduction)

Chimaera was a fire-breathing monster, part lion, part dragon and part goat. Gyas was a giant.

In I.11 Horace advised Leuconoe to ignore astrology. Here, he himself refers to favourable signs of the zodiac. For Saturn opposing Jupiter, see II.12. Maecenas' recovery from illness and the applause in the theatre is referred to in I.20. Horace's experience with the tree is the subject of II.13. Mercury seems to have protected both poets and bankers, and is the subject of I.10 and III.11, as well as being credited with the rescue of Horace from the battlefield of Philippi in II.7.

II.18

Hymettus was a mountain near Athens, noted for its honey and its marble. Attalus III of Pergamos was famous for his wealth and was said to have invented the art of weaving fabric from gold.

For the developments around Baiae, compare II.15 and III.1.

Orcus, the underworld, is also used as a name for Pluto its king. His accomplice in this case could be either Mercury (see last stanza of I.10) or the ferryman Charon (see last stanza of II.3). For Prometheus and Tantalus, see II.13.

II.19

Bacchus, the son of Semele (see I.19), was the god of wine, ecstasy and the irrational. Liber, the old Roman god of wine and fruit, became identified with him. The thyrsus was Bacchus' magical staff, around which ivy and vine-shoots were twined. Thyiades were Bacchantes, women who honoured the god by celebrating ecstatic mysteries on the hillsides.

Ariadne, the daughter of Minos of Crete, rescued Theseus from the labyrinth and returned with him to Greece. Theseus abandoned her at Naxos, where Bacchus fell in love with her. According to different versions, he made Ariadne or her crown into a constellation.

Pentheus, king of Thebes, repressing the irrational side of his nature, was disgusted at the Bacchantes' celebrations. He refused to succumb to Bacchus' assaults on his city, and, clothed in an animal skin, spied on the Bacchantes. They, inspired by Bacchus, tore him apart. The story is the subject of the *Bacchae* a drama by the Athenian Euripides in the fifth century BC.

Lycurgus, king of the Edonians in Thrace, prohibited the worship of Bacchus and ordered his subjects to destroy their vines. For this he was driven mad and killed his own son Dryas with an axe, believing him to be a vine, which he then proceeded to prune. At Bacchus' instigation, the Edonians took him to Mount Pangaeum and had his body pulled apart by wild horses. The Bistonids were Thracian Bacchantes.

Rhoetus was a giant who participated in the rebellion against Jupiter. The episode is referred to in III.4. Cerberus is the hound of II.13.

II.30

The story of Daedalus is also touched on in I.3. His son, Icarus, attempted to fly from the island of Crete, but the wax fastening his wings melted in the sun and he fell into the sea.

The Moroccan sands were the Syrtes, mentioned in I.22. Colchis, east of the Black Sea, was the home of Medea and the Golden Fleece of legend. Ukraine has been used, anachronistically, to translate the Latin reference to Gelonians, Rumania for Dacians, and Spain for Iberians.

For a swan as a bird representing a lyric poet, see IV.2, where Pindar is called "the swan of Dirce", and VI.3.

III.1

The first six odes of Book III are known as the Roman Odes, as all of them touch on aspects of Roman character, morality and tradition. They were intended to inspire the Augustan generation after years of civil war.

For Jove's conquest over the giants, see II.19 and III.4.

The Campus was the Campus Martius, which was not only the park and sports-ground referred to in I.8 and I.9, but the location where the elections of Rome's officials took place. The goddess Necessity features in I.35. For the urn containing the lots of destiny, see II.3. The drawn sword refers to the sword of Damocles, suspended above the subject's neck by Dionysus, a tyrant of Syracuse in Sicily. Tempe was the pretty Thessalian valley referred to in I.7. In October, the evening setting of Arcturus, the brightest star in the constellation Bootes, was believed to portend stormy weather. The kid-star rose in the evening at the same time of year.

The scene at the waterside recalls the references to Baiae in II.15 and II.18.

The image of black Anxiety in this ode is similar to that of false Care in II.16, causing some scholars to believe that II.16 contains an interpolation. The point of the image here is that anxiety stalks the property tycoon, whether he is on his luxury boat or riding off on his horse.

III.2

"*Dulce et decorum est pro patria mori,*" the words at the beginning of the fourth stanza, were repeated by Wilfred Owen, the poet of the First World War. The popular breeze of the fifth stanza is also a phrase immortalised by Horace. Manliness translates the Latin "*virtus*", which is often translated "virtue", but is derived from the word *vir* meaning man, and in the Augustan era properly refers to manly qualities. (In II.2, since the reference is to telling the truth, the word "virtue" has been used to translate the Latin).

Canoe is a deliberate anachronism for "phaselon", a Greek word imported by Horace, which signifies a light boat shaped like a bean.

III.3

Juno was the wife of Jove. Auster was the south wind. For Pollux, the brother of Castor, see I.3.

Augustus is again referred to as a god in IV.5, with more ambiguous references in I.2 and I.12. For nectar, see I.13.

Quirinus refers here to Romulus, the grandson of Juno and mythical founder of Rome. He was the son of Mars and Rhea Silvia. In spite of her hostility towards Romulus because of his mother, Juno allowed him to escape death by flying to heaven on Mars' horses.

Laomedon, king of Troy, was the father of Priam. He cheated Neptune and Apollo of their promised fee, when they built his city walls and tended his flocks, and defrauded Hercules by substituting mortal mares for the pair of immortal, snow-white mares he had promised Hercules for rescuing his daughter Hesione from a sea-monster.

Minerva was usually identified with the Greek goddess Pallas Athene, the virgin goddess of Athens (see I.7). Here, Minerva is a specifically Roman goddess. She is identified as a protectress of chastity who will care for Troy and her people, after the damage done to them by the Spartan adulteress Helen, and assist in relocating Trojan exiles in Rome. Priam, king of Troy, was the father of Paris who abducted Helen. The Achaeans, or Greeks, came to recapture her in the Trojan War, in which Hector fought heroically for the Trojans. For the poem's theme, compare I.15.

The Capitol can refer either to the Capitoline Hill itself or to the Temple of Jupiter Capitolinus on the hill. This was a centre of important symbolic significance in Rome. In ancient days there had been an Old Capitol on the Quirinal Hill, dedicated to Jupiter (Jove), Juno and Minerva. A purpose of the ode is to give legitimacy to Rome's origins, by linking them with the fall of Troy. Virgil attempted this with greater success in his Aeneid. In that epic work, written at the same period as Horace's odes, the hero Aeneas was a Trojan exile who epitomised Roman morality, self-denial and manliness, qualities which the authorities in the Augustan age were trying to restore.

The last stanza shows that Horace is aware that the grand rhetoric of his theme and delivery are not suited to his talents or to the style of lyric poetry, compare the ending of II.1.

III.4

This ode takes up the running from the last stanza of the previous ode. The Muse Calliope inspires Horace to recount some autobiographical detail, including four escapes from possible death and references to his favourite locations, before returning to heavier themes of myth and religion, which illustrate the supremacy of order and the inevitable punishment of the guilty and immoral.

Mount Voltur was about five miles west of Venusia, where Horace was born. Forentum, Bantia and Acherontia were neighbouring settlements. Praeneste (today's Palestrina) was a town east of Rome and beyond Tibur (todays's Tivoli), not far from Horace's farm in the Sabine hills. Baiae was on the coast and is referred to in a number of odes, where excessive building and land development are criticised. See II.15 and II.18.

Horace had escapes from death at Philippi, described in II.7; a falling tree, II.13; and a storm off Palinurus described here. Palinurus was a promontory on the toe of Italy, possibly today's Punto dello Spartimento.

Basques is an anachronistic translation of "*Concanus*", a savage tribe of northern Spain. Ukrainians translates the Latin "*Geloni*", a nomadic tribe.

Pierian refers to a mountain in Thessaly sacred to the Muses.

The Titans and Giants rebelled unsuccessfully against Jove and other gods for supremacy in heaven. Otus and Ephialtes were the brothers who tried to drop Mount Pelion on the top of Olympus. They were sons of Iphimedeia by Neptune, and grew one fathom in height and one cubit in breadth every year, declaring war on Olympus, the home of the gods, when they were nine years old. They were tricked to their death by Diana in the form of a white doe. Aiming to kill her, they shot one another with their spears.

Typhoeus was killed by Jove's thunderbolt and buried under Mount Etna. Mimas, another giant, gave his name to a mountain range in Ionia opposite the isle of Chios. Porphyrion, Mimas and Rhoetus were also giants, the latter being mentioned in II.19.

Pallas is Pallas Athene, often identified with the Roman goddess Minerva. For Vulcan, see I.4. Castalia was a fountain on Mount Parnassus in Greece, and was sacred to Apollo and the Muses. Delos was an island in the Aegean sacred to Apollo. Patara was a sea-port of Lycia in Asia Minor with an oracle to Apollo.

For Gyas, see II.17. For Orion and Diana, see II.13. Etna is where Typhoeus was buried, see above. For Tityos, see II.14. Pirithous was king of the Lapiths and husband of Hippodamia. After Hippodamia's death he descended to the underworld with Theseus, planning to carry off its queen Proserpine, but was seized and put in chains. The description "lover" refers to Pirithous' attempt on Proserpine, and not solely, if at all, to his love for Hippodamia. Faunus' love in III.18 is of the same variety.

Crassus, a member of the First Triumvirate with Pompey the Great and Julius Caesar, was keen to match their military achievements and prestige. Invading Parthia in 53 BC with a force of 35,000 men, his infantry was destroyed by a Parthian force of 10,000 archers. Crassus was killed ingloriously. Only ten thousand Romans escaped. The rest, who survived the battle, were carried off into captivity.

Marsians and Apulians were troops from the Italian provinces with a reputation for toughness. The sacred shields were ancient Roman relics held in the Temple of Mars.

Marcus Atilius Regulus was a Roman consul in 256 BC during the First Punic War of 264-241 BC. He was sent with his fellow-consul Manlius Vulso, to beat off a Carthaginian naval threat against Sicily and, having won the battle of Cape Ecnomus, invaded Africa, only to be defeated at Bagradas. Regulus was sent back to Rome on parole by the Carthaginians, to negotiate a settlement in Sicily, but advised against compromise and returned to his captors.

III.6

This is the last of the six Roman Odes. Hesperia, in this context, refers to Italy.

Monaeses and Pacorus were Parthian commanders; Monaeses defeated the Roman forces in Syria in 36 BC, and Pacorus won a series of victories around 40 BC before being killed in 38 BC. The victorious Parthians took gold rings off the fingers of their dead foes and wore them on their necklaces.

The Ethiopians were troops of the Egyptian Cleopatra, see I.37. The Dacians also sided with Mark Antony against Octavian. Ionia refers to Asia Minor, with its supposed moral laxity.

The Carthaginian blood was spilled in the naval victory off Sicily in the First Punic War, see III.5. Pyrrhus was a king of Epirus, who invaded Italy in 280 BC. Antiochus was defeated by the Roman general Scipio Africanus in 190 BC. Hannibal was the Carthaginian general who invaded Italy with his elephants in the Second Punic War of 218-202 BC.

In the classical world of Greece and Rome, it was believed that the golden age was in the past, by contrast with the Judaeo-Christian belief that a better age is to come.

III.7

Oricum was an Adriatic port south of today's Brindisi. Asterie's love, in Horace's Latin, is named as Gyges and could be, but is not necessarily, the Gyges of II.5. Chloe is the name of the local hostess in Oricum.

Proteus was a mythical king of Tiryns. His wife, Anteia, sometimes known as Stheneboea, fell in love with Bellerophon. When Bellerophon rejected her advances, she told her husband he had tried to seduce her, whereupon Proteus sent him with a sealed letter to Anteia's father, Iobates, king of Lycia, which read: "Please remove the bearer from this world; he has tried to violate my wife, your daughter." Bellerophon rode on the winged horse Pegasus to Iobates' palace, killing the Chimaera on the way, and Iobates sent him on a series of dangerous missions, but Bellerophon survived victorious. Iobates eventually discovered the truth, when Bellerophon ran away rather than succumb to the advances of the local women. He then gave Bellerophon his daughter Philonoe in marriage.

The wife of Acastus of Iolcus, called Hippolyte here, but elsewhere known as Cretheis, tried to seduce Peleus who had fled to Iolcus from Aegina. Acastus challenged him to a hunting contest, but Peleus had a magic sword and won. Acastus hid the sword and arranged for the Centaurs to kill Peleus as he slept at a banquet, but Cheiron the king of the Centaurs saved his life and found his sword. This Hippolyte is not the Amazon wife of Theseus, but came from Magnesia in Thessaly.

The Campus Martius, adjoining a bend in the Tiber, was used for sports, riding and athletics, see I.8, I.9 and III.1.

III.8

The point to Maecenas' imagined question was that the first of March was usually celebrated by married women. This was the date of the *Matrimonalia*, a holiday on which Juno was honoured.

Liber, identified with Bacchus, is credited with saving Horace from the falling tree of II.13. In II.17 Faunus is given the credit.

Lucius Volcacius Tullus was consul in 66 BC. This would nearly coincide with Horace's birth in 65 BC, and a wine from that year is the subject of III.21. Alternatively, Lucius Volcacius' son was consul in 33 BC. Wine was often stored in a small room over the hearth. It was thought that the smoke and warmth helped the ageing process, as well as ensuring that the wine was of a suitable temperature for drinking.

Cotiso is referred to by the historian Suetonius as king of the Getians, a tribe who lived by the Danube and were often confused with the Dacians from today's Rumania. Cotiso could have been the king of the northern shore of I.26. The reference to civil strife among the Parthians may also be echoed in I.26; Tiridates, supported by Augustus, was hostile to Phraates IV. Augustus was absent from Rome on his Spanish campaign from 26-24 BC, and Parthian resistance continued until suppressed by Agrippa in 19 BC. In Augustus' absence Maecenas carried much responsibility for Rome's affairs. The Scythians were nomads from the plains north of the Black Sea. For Horace's sentiments, compare III.29.

III.9

Ilia, a name which denotes a Trojan origin, was Rhea Silvia, the mother of Romulus, mentioned in Juno's declaration of III.3. Calais is pronounced in three syllables. He was the son of Ornytus from Thurii, or Thurium, on the gulf of Tarentum in southern Italy.

Lydia occurs in I.8, I.13 and I.25. In III.26 we learn that Chloe is from Thrace. Chloe is depicted as a frightened deer in I.23. The sea of Hadria is the Adriatic.

III.10

An old Lyce occurs in IV.13. The Tanais was today's river Don. Penelope was the wife of Odysseus, whose kingdom was the island of Ithaca off western Greece. During the twenty year period between his departing for and returning from the Trojan War, she held off her wooers by never completing a shroud she was weaving.

Maecenas was Etrurian, or Etruscan; perhaps the reference to Etrurian gentry contains a veiled compliment to him.

The adjective "Thessalian" translates the Latin "*Pieria*", see III.4. As the Muses came from the Pierian part of Thessaly, there is an implication that the lover of Lyce's husband could be a musician.

III.11

The theme of this ode is the explanation to Lyde of the loyalty required of a wife. This may not be the Lyde of III.28, who seems to be servant, musical companion and, probably, lover.

Amphion was the son of Antiope, who was seduced by Jove and gave birth to twin boys, the other being Zethus. When the boys grew up, they visited Thebes, their mother's birthplace, ejected the king and rebuilt the walls of the lower city. Amphion had been given a lyre by the god Mercury, who had invented the original lyre and presented it to Apollo. Zethus taunted Amphion for allowing it to distract him from work, but when they began to build, Amphion's stones moved to the sound of his lyre and slid into place.

An inverted, scooped-out tortoiseshell formed the body of the lyre. Originally lyres had four strings, but a seven-string lyre was developed around 650 BC, supposedly by Terpander of Corinth, and contributed to the flowering of Greek lyric poetry at that time.

The theme of the young girl as filly echoes the heifer of II.5 and the deer of I.23.

Cerberus is described in II.13, where the Eumenides, synonymous with the Furies, are also mentioned.

Ixion was the son of Phlegyas, the Lapith king. He murdered Eioneus, his prospective father-in-law, but Jove consented to purify him and invited him to dinner. Ixion, ungratefully, planned to seduce Juno, but Jove was suspicious and created a false Juno out of cloud. As Ixion took his pleasure with the cloud, Jove surprised him and had him bound to a wheel of fire which rolled ceaselessly through the sky.

Tityos had attempted to violate Diana. His punishment is described in III.4 and he is also referred to in II.14.

Danaus, who had originally been king of Libya, later became such a powerful king in Greece that future generations were often called Danaans. He built the citadel of Argos and had fifty daughters. His twin brother Aegyptus, after whom Egypt was named, had fifty sons. After their father's death the brothers quarrelled, but it was eventually agreed that the cousins should marry in a mass wedding. Aegyptus' sons planned to murder their brides, but Danaus armed his daughters with sharp pins to hide in their hair and instructed them to kill their husbands at midnight. However, Hypermnestra saved the life of Lynceus because he had spared her virginity. Her sisters were condemned as a result of the murders to the endless task of carrying water in the underworld in leaky jars. Horace's version omits the murderous plan of Aegyptus' sons, focussing on the crime of the Danaus' daughters. The reference to Venus, the Queen of Love, in the last stanza also implies that Horace plays down the question of Hypermnestra's virginity in favour of a more dutiful yet romantic concept of marriage.

III.12

This translation reflects the unusual metre of the original ode, the rare *Ionicus a minore*. The name Neobule is derived from the Greek and suggests new-fangled ideas. Hence the term "stupid" in the second stanza.

Bellerophon was the rider of Pegasus, see III.7.

III.13

The location of the spring of Bandusia has not been positively identified, but is likely to be in the Sabine hills near Horace's farm. Libations of wine and offerings of flowers were offered to springs at the festival of *Fontinalia*. The Dog-days in this instance refer to the rising of the constellation Canicula, or Lesser Dog, at the end of July.

III.14

Hercules represents a mythical parallel to Augustus, as he, too, came to Italy from Spain after a victory, in his case over Geryon, see II.14. Augustus returned to Rome after his Spanish campaign in the summer of 24 BC. The fact that this ode is addressed to the "*plebs*", the common people of Rome, may be significant. Augustus faced some opposition from sections of the Roman aristocracy at this time (see II.10 and Introduction).

Augustus' wife was Livia, mother by her first marriage of the future emperor Tiberius. See also note IV.14. Augustus' sister was Octavia, the mother by her first husband of Marcellus, who was exposed to public criticism in the Murena scandal of 23 BC, and who died shortly thereafter.

The bands of prayer, or chaplets, were worn around the head. The Marsian War, a war in Italy itself between Romans and Marsians, as a result of which Rome won control of the peninsula, took place in 90 BC. Spartacus led the slave rebellion of 73 to 71 BC. Munatius Plancus, the addressee of I.7 was consul in 42 BC, the year of the Battle of Philippi. Horace hints to his audience that it was youthful impetuosity that caused him to fight, and fight on the wrong side, too.

III.15

Chloris figures briefly in II.5 where her white shoulder glimmers in the moonlight. Pholoe, apart from an even briefer reference in the same ode, is the abrasive girl of I.33. Luceria, the modern Lucera, was where the finest Italian wool was produced.

III.16

Acrisius had a single daughter Danae, but no male heir. When he asked the oracle how to remedy this, he was told he would have no sons, but that his grandson would kill him. For this reason he imprisoned Danae, but Jove came in a shower of gold and Perseus was born, the slayer of Medusa the Gorgon. Years later, Perseus inadvertently killed his grandfather at some funeral games in Larissa. His discus struck his grandfather's foot, and the old man died from the injury.

The Argive prophet was Amphiaraus, the brother-in-law of Adrastus the king, whose small group of famous warriors set out in a disastrous campaign known as the Seven against Thebes, the subject of an early Greek tragedy by the playwright Aeschylus. Amphiaraus' wife, Eriphyle, was bribed by the promise of a magic necklace to persuade her husband to join the expedition. After his death, she was killed by her son and he was pursued by the Furies for her murder.

The Macedonian was Philip II, the father of Alexander the Great. He reigned in the late fifth century BC and was notorious for his bribes. It has been suggested that the reference to captains of frigates could contain an oblique criticism of Menas, a naval commander under Octavian's enemy Sextus Pompeius in the period around 36 BC; Menas who twice reneged on commitments to Octavian.

After their year in the consulate, consuls became proconsuls, usually being appointed as governors of Rome's overseas provinces. Calabria is in southern Italy. Laestrygonia, mentioned in Homer's Odyssey, was later identified with the Italian Formiae. Mygdon was a legendary prince of Phrygia, while the kingdom of Alyattes, the father of Croesus, was the adjacent territory of Lydia, both in Asia Minor.

III.17

The name Lamia also occurs in I.26 and I.36. All three references may be to the senior praetorian legate responsible for three or four legions based in Tarragona in Spain from 24 to 22 BC. Lucius Aelius Lamia was a contemporary of Horace, having been born in the same year, 65 BC.

Lamus appears in Book 10 of Homer's Odyssey and this reference gives the Lamia family the sort of pedigree that appealed to Romans in the Augustan age.

Formiae was a town near the coast between Rome and Naples where the river Liris flowed into the sea. Marica was a nymph, who was sometimes known as the mother of the Latins.

The Latin makes clear that the pork will be sucking pig, just two months old.

III.18

Faunus, already mentioned in I.4, was the protecting deity of shepherds and agriculture in Latium, the ancient country around Rome. Later he was identified with the Greek Pan, and represented with horns and goats' feet (see I.4). The love he offered to the Nymphs was similar to that of Pirithous in III.4, lust rather than affection. The deep bowl was Venus' friend because wine was thought to assist love-making. The special December day was the Nones, which fell on the fifth of the month.

III.19

As in I.27, the scene is a drinking party. Telephus occurs in I.13 as the violent young man whom Lydia loves.

Inachus was the first king of Argos, and Codrus was the last king of Athens, who gave himself voluntarily to death in order to give his people victory over the Spartans. Aeacus was the grandfather of Achilles, and said to have been the ancestor of the kings of Macedon. Ilium was an alternative name for Troy.

Chian wines were produced on the Aegean island of Chios. As with much wine of this period, water was often added. In III.17 wine is also heated. The Apennines were a mountain range running down the centre of Italy.

Murena may be the Licinius of II.10, often believed to be the Licinius Varro Murena, who was the brother of Maecenas' wife Terentia, and who met his death through his involvement in a plot against Augustus in 23 BC. He is toasted here on his entry to the College of Augurs, a magistracy open to men of aristocratic birth.

The poet is arguing artificially, in the interests of a good party, that thrice three conforms with the gracious limit of three, whereas nine would be too much. Graces occur in I.4, I.30 and III.21.

Berecyntia is a name given to Cybele, see I.18. The Berecyntian pipe is a curved flute from Phrygia, see also IV.1

Glycera appears in I.19, I.30, I.33 and III.19.

III.20

Pyrrhus is given little chance by Horace of winning the love of Nearchus in the face of opposition from the lioness. Nireus was a young Greek warrior in the Trojan War, known for his looks. Ganymede, a youth of exceptional beauty, was, as described in IV.4, snatched by the eagle on Mount Ida and taken to heaven, where he became Jove's cupbearer.

III.21

The wine is from the vintage of 65 BC, the year of Horace's birth when Lucius Manlius Torquatus was consul. The first few lines of the ode are in a mock-religious style, mirroring the ritual invocation to a deity.

Corvinus' full name was Marcus Valerius Messalla Corvinus. He had been a student in Athens with Horace and, like Horace, had joined Brutus' forces. He later supported Octavian and commanded part of his fleet at the Battle of Actium. A noted orator, he was a patron of the poet Tibullus, the addressee of I.33, and he was celebrated for his drinking. For Cato, see II.15. Wine-drinking was not considered inconsistent with traditional Roman virtues.

III.22

Diana's triple form arises from her earthly role as the goddess of hunting, her heavenly role as the moon-goddess, and her underworld role as Hecate, who was often represented with three heads. The pine-tree is here identified with Diana, and the sacrifice is to both goddess and tree.

III.23

The gods in the first stanza are the Lares, the tutelar deities of the home, who originated in the ancient Etruscan religion. Mount Algidus was in the Alban hills, south of Rome (see I.21). A pontifex was a high priest. In the last stanza, the gods of home are the Penates, the Latin gods of the household, who are to be appeased by the ritual scattering of flour and the throwing of salt onto the fire. Both sets of gods would be represented by small idols and would remain with the family if they moved house (see II.18).

III.24

The reference to the seas being filled with debris recalls the scene in II.18. The goddess Necessity is also described in I.35, where she is a slave and companion to Fortuna. The nomadic Scythians and the Getae, who lived on the Danube, are here depicted as representing the old virtues. The Capitol, in this context, refers to the location of the public treasury. The ode repeats some of the themes of the Roman Odes, III.1-6. For the vocabulary of banking in the last line, see I.9.

III.25

For Bacchante, see III.15. The Bacchantes' power to uproot trees in their frenzy is referred to in Euripides' play *The Bacchae*, For Hebrus, see I.25. Rhodope was a mountain range, also in Thrace. Naiads were fresh-water nymphs.

The god divine, whom the inspired poet follows, can perhaps be taken to imply Augustus as well as Bacchus himself.

III.26

A military metaphor is used to describe the lover who retires from active service. Scholars have often commented that the equipment to be laid down would have been used to storm the doors of a would-be mistress's house, even though torches, crowbars and bows make an unlikely combination for such a purpose; they have ignored the possibility of these being sexual images signalled by the reference to Venus.

Venus' home in Cyprus is referred to in I.30. She also had a temple in Memphis in Egypt. Chloe, who we know from III.9 to have been flaxen-haired, came from Sithone in Thrace. Her northern blasts are contrasted with Venus' warmth. Venus normally used her whip to drive her victims beneath the yoke, also alluded to in III.9.

III.27

Galatea is returning to Greece, probably via the port of Brindisi, so she rides out of Rome along the Via Appia, passing Lanuvium on the west. Horace recites the names of four birds regarded in Roman practice as ill-omened. The *parra* is here translated as barn-owl, but scholars have also rendered it as lapwing or green woodpecker. The other birds are: *corvus*, raven; *picus*, woodpecker; *cornix*, crow. The left, or sinister, hand was considered unlucky. For Orion, which set in early November, see also I.28. Iapyx, also referred to in the context of Virgil's voyage to Athens in I.3, was the west/north-westerly wind which blew from Italy to Greece. Auster was the southern wind, which came from the direction of Rome's traditional and more recent enemies, the Carthaginians and the Egyptians; hence, the poet's train of thought leading to the introduction of the Europa myth.

Europa, the daughter of Agenor, was born near Tyre. Jove fell in love with her and disguised himself as a beautiful and gentle snow-white bull, allowing her to put garlands on his horns and flowers in his mouth. However, once she had climbed on his back, he swam with her to Crete, where he ravished her. The continent named after her was, of course, Europe.

III.28

Lyde is the name of the obdurate young filly of III.11, who was told the cautionary tale of the daughters of Danaus. Here, she is a servant, musical companion and, probably, lover.

Caecubum in southern Latium produced a particularly fine wine. Bibulus was consul in 59 BC, so the vintage dates to that year. The pun (bibulous) is intended in Latin as in English.

The *Neptunalia*, or holiday of Neptune, was on 23 July. The singing would start with a song in Neptune's honour. The Nereides were his sea-nymphs. Lato, or Latona, was the mother of Apollo and Diana. Diana was sometimes known as Cynthia after Mount Cynthus on Delos, where she and her brother were born, just as Apollo could be called Cynthius (see I.21)

Cnidos was a city in Caria in Asia Minor, where a statue of Venus stood, carved by the brilliant Athenian sculptor of the fifth century BC, Praxiteles (see also I.30). The Cyclades were the islands around Delos in the Aegean Sea. Paphos was a city on the island of Cyprus, which was sacred to Venus and had a famous temple of the goddess.

III.29

A similar introduction to Maecenas appears at the beginning of I.1. The ben-nut, grown in the Middle East, produced a sweet-smelling oil, which was used for body-lotion and hair-dressing.

For Tibur, today's Tivoli, see I.7. Aufula was between Tibur and Praeneste, referred to in III.4. Telegonus was the son of Ulysses and Circe; he is referred to in I.17, and is not to be confused with Telemachus, the son of Ulysses and his wife Penelope. Telegonus, having reached manhood, went in search of his father. He sailed to

Ithaca, which he mistook for Corcyra, and attacked Ulysses without knowing him, killing him with a spear tipped with the spine of a sting-ray. Telegonus later founded Tusculum in the Alban hills south-east of Rome. Ulysses was the Roman name for the Greek Odysseus.

Maecenas had a magnificent mansion on the Esquiline Hill in Rome and was known for his lavish lifestyle. For Horace's sentiments, see III.8.

Andromeda was the daughter of King Cepheus of Ethiopia, who had her bound to a rock, where she was rescued from a sea-monster by Perseus, who then married her. All three were finally placed among the stars. Procyon was the major star of the Lesser Dog, which rose before the Dog Star itself. The expression "the dog days of summer" refers to the hot weather at their rising.

Silvan, or Silvanus, was the god of forests and thickets. Tanais occurs in III.10 and is now known as the river Don. Cyrus' realm was in Asia Minor. For the goddess Fortuna, see I.35.

The Twins are Castor and Pollux, the guiding stars of sailors (see I.3 and IV.8). Their temple in Rome was first dedicated in 484 BC.

III.30

The north-wind was known as Aquilo. Death's goddess was called Libitina. Both these Latin names are used by Horace in the original. The Capitol housed the Temple of Jupiter Capitolinus in Rome.

In IV.9 we learn that Horace was born near the river Aufidus, which flowed down from the mountain country of Apulia. Venusia, the town of his birth, was about ten miles distant. Daunus was the legendary first king of Apulia and is called waterless because of its arid climate.

Aeolian refers to the odes of Alcaeus and Sappho, because their songs were written and sung in the Aeolian dialect of Greek. The Delphic laurel is the laurel or bay of Apollo, the god of lyric poetry, whose shrine and oracle were at Delphi, and the phrase has resonances of victories in the Pythian games which were celebrated in Delphi every four years.

Just as I.1, the prologue, concludes with a reference to Euterpe and Polyhymnia, so III.30, the epilogue of the three-volume publication of 23 BC, ends with a reference to Melpomene, the Muse of lyric poetry.

IV.1

Cinara had been a lover of Horace in earlier life. Her premature death is referred to in IV.13.

Paullus Fabius Maximus came from a distinguished family and a chapter in Syme's "The Augustan Aristocracy" is devoted to him (Ch.XXVIII). This ode is in celebration of Paullus' forthcoming marriage to Augustus' first cousin Marcia. Syme suggests the ode was written around 16 BC; Paullus became consul in 11 BC.

The Alban lake was south of Rome (see III.23). For Berecyntian, see I.18 and III.19. The Salians (or "Leapers") were a college of priests in Rome, who sang and danced around the city and its holy places in the first half of March of each year. See also I.36. For Ligurinus, see IV.10.

IV.2

Iullus Antonius was the son of Mark Antony and his first wife, Fulvia. Iullus did not suffer as a result of his father's hostility to Octavian and his subsequent defeat, but was brought up by Augustus' sister Octavia, who had been Mark Antony's second wife. Iullus had a distinguished career, becoming consul in 10 BC.

For Daedalus, see I.3. The Icarian sea was named after his son Icarus. Pindar was one of the earliest and greatest of the Greek lyric poets. Dirce was a fountain in Thebes. The swan of Dirce is Pindar. For this image, see II.20 and IV.3.

For Centaurs, see I.18 . For Chimaera, see I.27. The Centaurs were killed by Pirithous (the lover of III.4), Chimaera by Bellerophon (see III.12). Orcus is the underworld or its king, Pluto.

Mount Matinus was in Apulia where Horace was born (see I.28). Tibur is the modern Tivoli, the nearest town to Horace's Sabine farm. He is believed to have had a house there in later life.

The Sacred Way led into Rome from the east towards the Capitol and was part of the triumphal route. The Sygambrians were a German tribe.

IV.3

This ode was probably written after Horace had been commissioned by Augustus to compose the Centennial Hymn, see Introduction and IV.6.

Melpomene was the Muse of lyric poetry, to whom the final words of III.30 are addressed. The Isthmian Games were celebrated at Corinth. An Achaean car was a two-wheeled racing chariot designed along traditional Greek lines. Delian foliage refers to garlands of laurel, sacred to Apollo of Delos. Aeolian songs were the lyric poems of the Greek poets of Asia Minor and its Aegean islands who wrote in the Aeolian dialect. For Pierian, see III.4. For swan, see also II.20 and IV.2.

IV.4

This ode was commissioned by Augustus to celebrate the victories in their Alpine campaigns of his stepsons Drusus, who died prematurely, and Tiberius, who later became emperor. Augustus and Livia had no children, but Augustus had a daughter Julia by his marriage to Scribonia. Livia's two sons, of whom Tiberius was the elder, were from her marriage to Tiberius Claudius Nero.

The Vindelici were a German tribe based on the modern Augsburg, see also IV.14.

In 207 BC Caius Claudius Nero led an extended forced march to the river Metaurus in north-east Italy to join battle against the Carthaginian Hasdrubal. The victory was regarded as a crucial turning point in the Second Punic War. Hasdrubal was the brother of the great Hannibal.

Eurus was the south-east wind. The Ausonian sea was between the Iapygian peninsula of southern Italy and the Straits of Sicily. Mount Algidus, south-east of Rome, is now Monte Compatri.

The Hydra was a mythical water-monster killed by Hercules. It originally had seven heads, but when one was cut off, another two grew in its place. Colchis was the home of Medea. There, Jason and the Argonauts were confronted with two fire-breathing bulls, which Jason had to subdue so as to perform his task of sowing a serpent's teeth; these, when planted in the ground, turned into armed men. The dragon of Thebes is surrounded by a similar myth. When it was slain by Cadmus, the goddess Athene (the Roman Minerva) ordered Cadmus to sow its teeth. Armed men sprang up, but Cadmus trickeded them into brawling among themselves. Echion was one of five survivors. Augustus' stepsons were from the Claudian *gens*, or tribe.

IV.5

Like Alexander the Great of Macedonia three hundred years earlier,
Augustus may have laid some claim to being divine. In his case it would
have arisen partly from the official apotheosis of Julius Caesar, his
adoptive father. The name Augustus itself and its Greek translation
Sebastos also implied a degree of divinity. For Romulus, see III.3.
Augustus had been absent on a military campaign.

The Carpathian sea was in the southern Aegean between Crete and
Rhodes. Ceres was the goddess of agriculture, particularly of cereal
crops. For unmarried trees, see II.15. Libations were poured to the gods
in the second course of a meal.

IV.6

Horace, having been given the honour by Augustus of composing the
Carmen Saeculare, or Centennial Hymn, for the Centennial Games in
Rome (see Introduction), prays to Phoebus Apollo for his support. The
ode becomes a rehearsal for the poet's young performers. See also IV.3.

Niobe, the wife of king Amphion of Thebes (see III.11), had seven sons
and seven daughters. Because she boasted of her superiority over the
goddess Latona, who had only two children, Apollo and Diana, she was
punished. Apollo and Diana shot all of her fourteen children dead with
arrows. Niobe herself was turned into a weeping stone, which some still
identify with a rock near Mount Sipylus in Turkey.

For Tityos, see II.14. Phthia in Thessaly was the birthplace of Achilles.
For Thetis, his mother, see I.8.

The story of the Trojan Horse is well known. Minerva was equivalent to
the Greek Pallas Athene. Aeneas, the son of Venus, was the legendary
founder of Rome celebrated by Horace's contemporary, Virgil, the
author of the Aeneid.

Thalia was one of the Muses. Xanthus was a river in Lycia. Camena
was the Roman Muse. For Daunus, see III.30. Delos' goddess was
Diana, just as its god was her brother Apollo. Both were children of
Latona. The Night-shiner was Diana in her form as the moon-goddess,
see III.22.

The Sapphic metre, named after Sappho the poetess of Lesbos, was the
metre of this ode in its original Latin.

IV.7

Torquatus was the last known member of the distinguished Manlius family, aristocrats who had seen their last consul in the year of Horace's birth, see III.21. Several members of the family were killed during the civil wars, some fighting for Pompey the Great. Torquatus himself did not seek political honours, preferring an unobtrusive life.

For Aeneas, see IV.6. Tullus and Ancus were the third and fourth of the legendary kings of ancient Rome. Minos was the son of Jove and Europa, and became a judge in the underworld. Hippolytus' stepmother Phaedra fell in love with him; when her advances were repelled, she accused him to her husband Theseus. A play on this theme was written by the Athenian dramatist Euripides, which still survives. Diana was the goddess of chastity. For Pirithous, see III.4.

IV.8

Censorinus is probably the Caius Marcius Censorinus who was consul in the year of Horace's death and died as a proconsular governor in the east, but could be his father who was consul in 39 BC.

Scopas and Parrhasius were a well-known Greek sculptor and painter.

Scipio brought the Second Punic War to a decisive end at the Battle of Zama in 202 BC, and was given the name Scipio Africanus. The Muses of Calabria are a reference to the old Roman poet Ennius, the author of the Annals, which celebrated the war. He was born in Calabria.

Mars's son was Romulus, who became, according to this story, founder of Rome. Aeacus was one of the judges in the underworld, which lay across the river Styx.

IV.9

Marcus Lollius came from a non-aristocratic family and was therefore a "*novus homo*", or new man. However, he rose to be consul in 21 BC. Because of his origins he may have been particularly anxious for recognition through an ode of Horace.

The names in the second and third stanzas are of Greek lyric poets. Ceos was an island off Cape Sunium at the tip of Attica. For Teucer and Sthenelus, see I.15. Idomeneus, king of Crete, led the Cretan contingent against Troy. Deiphobus was a son of Priam and Hecuba of Troy, and. according to one legend, married Helen after Paris's death. Hector was the great Trojan hero of the war. Agamemnon, king of Mycenae and leader of all the troops of Greece, was the brother of Menelaus, the husband of Helen.

IV.10

The first reference to Ligurinus is at the end of IV.1. Firm evidence of homosexual desire on Horace's part is only apparent in these two odes, both written after he reached the age of fifty. It has been suggested that there homosexual undertones in I.37 and II.5.

IV.11

After Book III, which was published just before Maecenas fell from political power, no odes were formally addressed to him by Horace, but this ode to Phyllis shows that Horace still had affection and regard for him. The Ides of April, the date of Maecenas' birthday, fell on the thirteenth. April was connected with Venus of the Sea, because the name of the month was thought to be derived from the Greek word *aphros*, meaning foam.

The name Telephus occurs also in I.13 and III.19, but does not necessarily signify the same person.

Phaethon was the son of the sun-god. He lost control of his father's horses and was destroyed by Jove to prevent the destruction of the earth. For Bellerophon, see III.12. After killing the Chimaera, he tried to fly to heaven on the winged horse Pegasus, but was thrown off.

IV.12

Other odes addressed to the poet Virgil are at I.3 and I.24.

Itys was the son of Tereus and Procne. Tereus, having fallen in love with Procne's sister Philomela, imprisoned his wife and cut out her tongue so that she could not communicate. However, Procne was released by Philomela, shocked at her own seduction. To punish her husband, Procne killed her son Itys and boiled him in a cauldron for Tereus to eat. Aghast at what he had been tasting, Tereus was on the point of killing the two sisters with an axe, when the gods changed Procne into a swallow, Philomela into a nightingale and Tereus himself into a hoopoe. Procne, as a daughter of Pandion, king of Athens, was a descendant of Cecrops, the first king of Attica.

Arcadia, a mountainous province in the Peloponnese, was noted for its idyllic beauty. Cales, now Calvi, was in southern Campania. Sulpicius is presumed to be a wine-merchant. Virgil, as Rome's greatest epic poet, will have found many willing patrons among the nobility.

Lyce occurs at III.10 and III.11. Chios was an Aegean island off the coast of Ionia in Asia Minor. The island of Cos was off the coast of Caria, one of the Sporadic islands in the Myrtoan Sea. Cinara is also mentioned in IV.1.

IV.14

This ode was commissioned by Augustus.

The "Senate and People of Rome" was the official title of the Roman Republic: "*Senatus Populusque Romanus*", which gave rise to the letters SPQR on Roman banners. The Vindelici were a German tribe based on the modern Augsburg, see IV.4. Latium was an early name for central Italy; hence, the language of Rome was called Latin.

Drusus was the stepson of Augustus, the son of his wife Livia. Born, according to the historian Suetonius, three months after her marriage to Augustus, Drusus is usually said to have been fathered by her first husband Tiberius Claudius Nero, but there were suspicions that Augustus was the natural father. Drusus' older brother, the Nero of the following stanza, was Tiberius, who later succeeded Augustus as emperor.

The Genaunians were a Germanic people in Raetia in the modern Val di Non. The Breunians were their neighbours.

The Pleiades were the constellation otherwise known as the Seven Stars, and were the daughters of Atlas and Pleione. For Daunus, see III.30. The reference to Alexandria recalls the defeat and death of Antony and Cleopatra, whose city surrendered on in August 30 BC. The Raetians seem to have surrendered to Tiberius Claudius exactly fifteen years later.

The Hister was the lower part of the river Danube. The Tigris flowed through the Parthian empire. The Sygambrians were a powerful German people, who lived between the Sieg and the Ruhr, and as far as the Lippe.

IV.15

This ode was commissioned by Augustus.

The Tyrrhenian seas were those off the Etruscan or west coast of Italy.

After the Roman military disaster at Carrhae in 53 BC, the Roman standards were captured by the Parthians, but their return was negotiated under Augustus. The doors of the Temple of Janus in Rome were closed during peace-time.

Julius Caesar and his adoptive son Augustus were both from the Roman clan known as *gens Julia*. Hence, Augustus' edicts were called Julian edicts.

The Getans, or *Getae*, were a Thracian tribe who lived near the Danube (see III.24). For Tanais, see III.10.

The reference to Lydian flutes expresses Horace's debt to the Greek lyric poets. Anchises was the father of Aeneas, whose mother was the goddess Venus. The last line of this last ode refers to the theme of Virgil's Aeneid, which is clearly the song which is to be sung. The Aeneid gave historical standing and legitimacy to Rome's claim to antiquity and pedigree, and supremacy both eastern and western empire.

Bibliography

Bibliography

Armstrong, David: **Horace**; *Yale University Press, 1989*

Cary, M.: **History of Rome**; *MacMillan, 1960 Edn.*

Grant, Michael: **The Roman Emperors (Augustus)**; *Weidenfeld and Nicolson, 1985.*

Graves, Robert: **The Greeks Myths**; *Penguin, 1962 edn.*

Highet, Gilbert: **Poets in a Landscape**; *Penguin, 1959 edn.*

Lonsdale, James, and Lee, Samuel: **Works of Horace, rendered into English prose**; *Macmillan, 1900.*

Nisbet, R.G.M.: ***Romanae Fidicen Lyrae*, The Odes of Horace (from J.P. Sullivan: Critical Essays on Roman Literature)**; *Routledge and Kegan Paul, 1962*

Quinn, Kenneth: **Horace–The Odes (introduction, text and commentary)**; *Nelson, 1980*

Scarre, Chris: **Historical Atlas of Ancient Rome**; *Penguin, 1995*

Suetonius: **Life of Horace**; *Harvard University Press, 1992 edn.*

Syme, Sir Ronald: **The Augustan Aristocracy**; *Clarendon Press, 1989 Edn.*

Syme, Sir Ronald: **The Roman Revolution**; *OUP, 1962 edn.*

West, David: **Horace Odes I, *Carpe Diem***; *OUP, 1995.*

Wilkinson, L.P.: **Horace and his Lyric Poetry**; *Bristol Classical Press, 1994 edn.*

INDEX

English first lines